Surviving the Japanese Onslaught

Surviving the Japanese Onslaught

An RAF PoW in Burma

A Biography of William Albert
Tate W.O. (Ret.) Royal Air Force
Bomber Command 1938–1946

William Tate M.A.

Pen & Sword
AVIATION

First published in Great Britain in 2016 by
Pen & Sword Aviation
an imprint of
Pen & Sword Books Ltd
47 Church Street
Barnsley
South Yorkshire
S70 2AS

ISBN 978 1 47388 073 3

A CIP catalogue record for this book is available from the British
Library

Typeset in Ehrhardt by
Mac Style Ltd, Bridlington, East Yorkshire
Printed and bound in the UK by CPI Group (UK) Ltd,
Croydon, CRO 4YY

Pen & Sword Books Ltd incorporates the imprints of Pen &
Sword Archaeology, Atlas, Aviation, Battleground, Discovery,
Family History, History, Maritime, Military, Naval, Politics,
Railways, Select, Transport, True Crime, and Fiction, Frontline
Books, Leo Cooper, Praetorian Press, Seaforth Publishing and
Wharncliffe.

For a complete list of Pen & Sword titles please contact
PEN & SWORD BOOKS LIMITED
47 Church Street, Barnsley, South Yorkshire, S70 2AS, England
E-mail: enquiries@pen-and-sword.co.uk
Website: www.pen-and-sword.co.uk

Contents

Dedication

During the twentieth century, in both the First and Second World Wars, millions of allied forces personnel and civilians made incalculable sacrifices; many of whom died or were wounded. Western nations and their allies fought to secure our heritage, values and lifestyle for the benefit not only of their own generation, but future generations too.

In the course of the two world wars members of my family and relatives rallied to the call to do what they believed was their duty. The First World War saw my paternal Grandfather, William, fight predominantly on the Western Front while my paternal Grandmother, Elizabeth (Stoker), worked in a munitions factory for part of the war. My maternal Grandfather, Arthur Cox, became a member of the Military Police, now the Royal Military Police, and served on the Western Front. Two of my Great Uncles, Lesley and Robert (Bob) Stoker also fought on the Western Front.

Throughout the Second World War my father served in the Royal Air Force (Bomber Command) and his younger brother Robert with the Royal Corps of Signals. My paternal Grandfather served in the Air Raid Precautions (Search & Rescue) and my paternal Grandmother joined the Nursing Auxiliary Service. My maternal Grandfather worked on the railways, which were vital for the transportation of troops, resources and equipment to keep the war machine operating. Two of my mother's brothers, Reginald and Ronald Cox, both served in the British Army. Reginald served in Europe and the Far East, and Ronald served in the Middle East. My aunt June, the wife of Roy Cox, lost her father when she was 4 years old. Her father, John Cook, was posted to the Far East in 1941 and subsequently captured by the Japanese. John died as a Prisoner of War in Kuching, in Sarawak in 1945.

Of the 55,573 personnel of Bomber Command who made the ultimate sacrifice in the Second World War, I wish to mention two veterans. First is Paul Griffiths, a Co-Pilot, who first befriended my father in the Middle East but later died as a Prisoner of War of the Japanese in Rangoon, Burma. Paul's death haunted my father for the rest of his life. Second is Douglas Jeffrey who, at the time of the war, was a Navigator who died during a mission over Germany. Douglas is the cousin of David and Flora Edwards, two wonderful friends to my parents and, understanding better than many why my father suffered a breakdown, remained supportive of the Tate family.

To my publishers, for their commitment, professional advice and applications I have depended on I sincerely and gratefully acknowledge the following staff: Laura Hirst (Aviation Imprint Commissioning Editor), Karyn Burnham (Sub-Editor), Charles Hewitt, Lori Jones, Jon Wilkinson, and Matthew Blurton.

Finally I pay respect to the thousands of medical personnel including doctors, physiotherapists, nurses, orderlies, administrative staff, surgeons, psychologists, psychiatrists, dentists and orthodontists who have healed, and continue to heal, many veterans in both body and mind.

It is to the above that I remain deeply, and humbly, beholden.

Introduction

After capture and interrogation, with several beatings on my face and other parts of my body over two days, I was taken outside where Japanese soldiers were then ordered to raise and aim their rifles at me; I stood stiffly to attention ... fearing the worst.

William A Tate: April 1943

It has been written of men who have undergone a cruel captivity ... that the record thereof has never faded from their countenances until they died.

Charles Dickens

In 1974, at 53 years of age, my father was admitted into hospital suffering a breakdown from a condition now extensively recognised as Post Traumatic Stress Disorder. This ailment resulted from William's incarceration between April 1943 and April 1945 as a Prisoner of War of the Japanese Imperial Forces in Rangoon Gaol in Burma (now Myanmar) during the Second World War. A number of symptoms associated with this illness William managed to control during the conflict and upon returning to civilian life, while others surreptitiously remained; nestled beneath the surface in a silent vigil, not spoken about, but waiting to erupt.

William was one of thousands of allied prisoners of war immutably scarred by the brutality and iniquitous butchery of their Japanese captors. This episode encompassed a systematic, intransigent policy of torture, beatings, solitary confinement, starvation, forced labour, insanitary and incommodious living quarters and virtually non-existent medical facilities and stores. These deeds gave rise to, or compounded, a profusion of health problems among prisoners including beriberi, dysentery, cholera, malaria, physical deformities, amputation of limbs without anaesthetic, tropical ulcers and other skin infections. The physical plight of the prisoners was encumbered by the unrelenting anguish of their minds, endured by all prisoners of Japanese Prisoner of War camps, and from which many predominantly young men, once healthy in mind, spirit and body, were never to return home to their cherished ones. The day my father was liberated from Japanese military forces, he had been reduced to an emaciated 6 st 2 lbs, (approximately 39 kg), less than half his normal weight, and with a nervous system entwined in a state of infirmity. In spite of this horrendous ordeal, William forever considered himself a fortunate man to have survived.

My intent in 2015, during the seventieth anniversary of the cessation of the war, where unpleasant personal opinions regarding Japan's war crimes may cause disapprobation, or be pressured into remaining hidden from the public domain, is to enlighten readers who may possess only a limited knowledge of the privations perpetrated by Japanese soldiers on their prisoners. These acts of callousness and cowardice, of a sanguinary disposition, did not belong to a civilised culture whatever apologia the Japanese people furnished Emperor Hirohito with, either preceding and during the war or, for that matter, in contemporary times.

Be they young or old, it is my desire that anyone who reads this biography, in part or whole, will further contemplate the details, though very personal from my perspective, as a timely and edifying recollection of some of the consequences pertaining to this abhorrent past.

The truth is, and generally persists today for the few remaining survivors of Japanese Prisoner of War camps, that much of the trauma forced on my father and his fellow prisoners could never heal. William's post-war torment afflicted him the remainder of his life. Those who knew my father may have glimpsed, but could never touch or feel in his gentle and intelligent eyes, the primary and secondary pains of 'the cross he had to bear.' William was one of many men and women intentionally ill-used. The repercussions extended to varying degree on William's beloved wife, other family members, friends and colleagues since these atrocities were committed. Innumerable lives were forever broken.

My father passed away on 11 February 2007 at the age of 85 and his epitaph, read to mourners at his funeral service, included one resonating sentiment that brings tears to my eyes. William wrote:

'Please do not weep for me–I am now in the deepest and most peaceful sleep I have ever known.'

In memory of my father and his fellow Prisoners of War of the Japanese.

'Fear no more the heat o' the sun,
Nor the furious winter's rages;
Thou thy worldly task hast done,
....
Thou art past the tyrant's stroke.'
William Shakespeare

William Tate: Son of the late William Albert Tate Esq.

Part I

Chapter 1

1938: Early RAF Days

Royal Air Force motto: *"Per ardua ad astra"* (Through adversity to the stars)

During the Second World War 55,573 Bomber Command Aircrew of the Royal Air Force made the ultimate sacrifice to defend Western democracy. This casualty rate was one of the highest of all the armed forces with approximately one in two personnel losing their lives. Those killed, whose average age was 22, included 38,462 Britons, 9,980 Canadians, 4,050 Australians and 1,703 New Zealanders.[1] Throughout the war Bomber Command flew more than 389,000 individual sorties from 101 operational bases across the east of England. Dozens more bases were built for training and maintenance.[2] Thousands more sorties by Allied forces were also conducted in the Middle East, Far East and Pacific Theatres of War against the enemy.

Winston Churchill once commented; 'Fighter Command won the Battle of Britain, but Bomber Command won the war.'[3] It has also been written many times that: 'the Bomber will always get through.' All RAF Bomber Aircrew were volunteers. The tremendous strains of operational flying affected all men to greater or lesser degrees – emotional exhaustion, operational-twitch, loss of nerve and shell shock were some of the symptoms but those in authority would not accept these descriptions and labeled such sufferers as having LMF (Lack of Moral Fibre). Officers were often dismissed in disgrace and NCOs (Non-Commissioned Officers) were reduced in rank, discharged, sent to the Navy or Army or put to work down coal mines. They were humiliated and vilified in the belief that other RAF personnel would think twice about trying to avoid combat duties. Thankfully, attitudes towards combat stress have greatly evolved during the twenty-first century.[4]

Not only were Bomber Command Aircrew all volunteers, the RAF also sought the best-educated personnel, with many coming from university and grammar schools. Numerous men and women were already enlisting in the armed forces as Volunteer Reservists prior to the official declaration of war on 3 September 1939. The Tate's eldest son, William Albert (Bill), was one of them. Following his studies at Woking County Grammar in 1937, Bill set his ambitions aside for a career in law and resigned as a Clerk from the law firm W Davies & Co. in 1938. People throughout Britain had been raised to revere and defend the values and heritage intrinsic to sustaining their way of life and be free from tyranny and dictatorship. A strong Christian ethos among the peoples of Western nations like Great Britain was also perhaps more noticeable in the 1930s.

Winston Churchill's warnings and concerns about Germany's rearmament policy were incompatible with many leaders who favoured, and adopted, a strategy of appeasement when confronting Hitler. The signing of a Tripartite Pact by Germany, Japan and Italy in September 1940, signaled an intolerable development and is now viewed by millions as a step closer to the destruction of democracy worldwide. The United States of America entered the war more than two years after hostilities began following Japan's attack on the US Pacific Fleet Base in Pearl Harbour, Hawaii, on the morning of 7 December 1941.

The circumstances that moved Bill to join the RAF were, in part, a patriotic duty to King and country. Throughout the war, King George VI and Queen Elizabeth, often referred to as the Queen Mother, constantly endeavoured to reassure British citizens, and encourage them to keep faith in victory over the enemy. When all was said and done the most obvious, and possibly only, solution was to stand and fight one's adversary.

Bill had been fascinated with aircraft and flying since childhood so this also influenced his decision. The potential of flight, both civil and military, had been recognised by politicians, scientists and aviation personnel during the First World War and the technology of aircraft was constantly being developed. Bill recalled that during 1938, his relationship with his father had deteriorated after a serious argument and, though Bill was very close to his mother, he realised that greater independence would be gained, at that point in time, by moving away from home.

Within a few weeks Bill had walked out of Number 10 Kirby Road in the then small village of Horsell, Surrey, with suitcase in hand. Bill's father and mother drove him to Woking station to catch an early morning train to London. He had already said his goodbyes to his younger brother Robert (Bob) and three sisters Ivy, Esther and Irene. His mother and father found it difficult to see their eldest son leaving home for the first time and felt the separation keenly. One of their many thoughts at this moment, as they stood on the platform waving goodbye, was a vague hope that hostilities with Germany might yet be avoided. Bill traveled to London on the day as requested to enlist with the Royal Air Force (Bomber Command). The date was Monday 7 November 1938. Having passed his physical test Bill signed his papers of enlistment after an examination of Mathematics and English. Subsequently he received his first uniform and Service Number: 625747. Apart from leave entitlements, Bill was now living away from home and so posted his civilian clothes back to his parents. Henceforth he was required to be in regulation uniform at all times.

Bill's initial experience as a raw recruit came with instructions to commence training at RAF Base Cardington, a village in Bedfordshire. These early weeks of basic training consisted of regular marching, (square bashing as Bill referred to it), rifle maintenance and target practice. By the time he had joined his first squadron, he had been issued with a Smith and Wesson pistol. Bill maintained his financial assistance to his family by regularly sending home part of his salary to his mother and with it a letter informing them of his experiences in the RAF.

Between March 1939 and September 1 1939 Bill was posted to Yatesbury in County Wiltshire for six months radio operation training at the RAF Yatesbury Training Centre. The accommodation was, as Bill recalled, basic 'huts' that each housed around twenty-eight recruits. The Trainee Wireless Operators Part of this course involved learning Morse code and Bill initially acquired a proficiency of twenty-five words per minute. With this came a basic understanding of key electronic components of the radio equipment. While at Yatesbury, Bill contracted measles and was forced to return home to Woking until he recovered putting him a few weeks behind with his schedule.

Life at Yatesbury was neither discomforting nor overly rigorous for the majority of new recruits. Bill considered the food served in the mess rooms relatively good. The main meal of the day often consisted of sausages or beef with vegetables. Supplies of most foods were still available until rationing in Britain started. Ration books, based on a points rationing system, were issued to citizens on January 8 1940 for items including butter, sugar and some meats. Government price controls and subsidies aimed to provide every citizen with basic essential products. When Bill started to make new friends at this base he and his fellow recruits would sometimes visit nearby sights of interest or go to local dances and pubs on their days off. Life for these young men being physically and mentally fit, and in the prime of their life, was relatively relaxed with few immediate worries.

Then came the news that people throughout Great Britain and many other countries had been dreading. War was declared on Sunday 3 September 1939 at 11.15 a.m. Millions of people throughout Britain tuned into their wirelesses as the Prime Minister Neville Chamberlain made an announcement to the public that:

'… this country is at war with Germany.'

Bill, like many other recruits, seemed to welcome the declaration and was enthusiastic to participate in hostilities against Germany. Like many of his fellow countrymen and women, Bill seemed positive at this stage that Britain and its allies could win the war although he would occasionally remember what his mother and father had experienced during the First World War.

His Majesty, King George VI, on the day World War Two was declared: Sunday, September 3, 1939, thus proclaimed:

I now call my people at home and my peoples across the seas who will make our cause their own. I ask them to stand calm, firm and united in this time of trial. The task will be hard. There may be dark days ahead and war can no longer be confined to the battlefield. But we can only do the right as we see the right and reverently commit our cause to God.

Regular discussions between RAF personnel increasingly focused on Germany's military plans and how Britain and its allies would respond. There were also numerous day to day relatively normal chats among recruits on many issues and topics including their families, wives and girlfriends, specific duties relative to recruits ranks and squadrons, current and new aircraft developments, the weather, films, music and of course, plans for the future when this war was over. As the Allied politicians seemed unable to halt

Germany's advances, first into Austria and then Poland, there remained the ever-present concern that Bill and his fellow recruits would be called upon to engage in hostilities.

On 4 November 1939, Bill was posted to RAF Evanton Base in Scotland for Air Gunnery Training. The defence of the Bomber from enemy fighter aircraft fell to the Air Gunner. This was considered an aircrew tradesman's role and Bill embarked on a four week intensive course using Westland Wallaces, Camera, Lewis and Vickers Gas Operated Guns. He passed the course and qualified on 1 December. Evanton today is a small village about six miles west of Invergordon on the north coast of the Cromarty Firth (Estuary) in the Highlands district of Ross and Cromarty. Between the village of Evanton and the eastern coast are some visible reminders of the hangars, buildings and runways of this former airfield used during the war. The aerodrome had been expanded in 1937. When Bill was stationed here, RAF Evanton was the farthest northerly station and became a base for flight and bomber training but principally Air Gunners. It was also used as a repair and bomb storage site. By 1943 the airfield was being used by RAF Coastal Command. Due to the short training schedule, Bill didn't have enough free time to visit the remote and mountainous western edge of Ross and Cromarty. He was devoting many hours studying the geography of maps of Western Europe and Britain, including weather patterns and known German military and industrial sites.

Chapter 2

1939: No. 38 Squadron

38 Squadron – Motto: *"Ante lucem"* (Before the dawn).

Badge: *A Heron Volant*. The Heron was chosen because this bird is found in great abundance in East Anglia, England where the unit was formed. Herons rarely miss their mark, become active as twilight descends, and are formidable fighters when attacked.[5]

The RAF and military planners needed trained, combat-ready crews to join various operational bomber squadrons as soon as possible. This did not take long. Within a week of completing Air Gunner training Bill received his first orders to join 38 Squadron based at Marham in Norfolk as a Wireless Operator and Air Gunner for his first Tour of Operations. In December 1938, the first of the new Vickers Wellington Bombers had been received by 38 Squadron, one of the few RAF Squadrons to use the Wellington for the duration of the war. The Vickers Wellington, popularly called 'The Wimpy' by service personnel after J Wellington Wimpy from the American Popeye cartoons, was a twin engine, medium bomber designed in the mid-thirties at Brooklands in Weybridge, Surrey and which Bill was partly familiar with from his early years of interest in aircraft. Bill occasionally travelled to this site and every so often would see a Wellington Bomber taking off and landing while it was still in its developmental stages.

Brooklands Airfield came under government control during the Second World War and by the end of the war in 1945, 2,515 Wellington Bombers had been built there along with Hawker Hurricane fighters. During the early years of the war, the Wellington was the main British Bomber and usually operated with a crew of five or six. More Wellington aircraft were built in Britain during the war than any other bomber and were the backbone of Bomber Command between 1939 and 1942. This aircraft served in virtually every Command of the RAF and became Britain's most successful twin-engine bomber. The Wellington was also the first bomber to strike at Germany (including Berlin), the first to drop the 4,000 lb 'Cookie Bomb' and to serve in every theatre of the war.[6] The new generation of larger, four-engine bombers such as the Avro Lancaster were designed and manufactured during 1942, along with advances in navigational technology, which allowed for the gradual phasing out of smaller aircraft. The Wellington Bomber however, because of its capabilities, remained in service until the 1950s.

Various versions of the Wellington appeared as the war progressed. Initially the bomber flew to heights ranging from 10,000 to 12,000 ft. The Mk III had four Browning guns; one on each beam side and similar guns in the nose and tail turrets with a 0.330 calibre and were capable of carrying a 4,000 lb bomb load. The Barnes Wallace (of Dam Buster fame) designed geodetic lattice-work fuselage construction made the Wellington a very sturdy, reliable and relatively light bomber which often survived battle damage that would have destroyed other aircraft. The Wellington Mk IC version with Pegasus engines became the standard for the RAF and had a flying ceiling to approximately 20,000 ft and speeds of around 410 km/h.[7] At these altitudes, and in sub-zero temperatures, flying was a very cold and uncomfortable journey for most bomber crews until further advances were developed in insulation and heating technology. Bill's thick fur lined leather Air Force jacket, which he kept after the war, gave him many years of service until it succumbed to long-term wear and tear and was finally discarded in the 1970s.

The town of Woking, located some thirty miles southwest of London, was bombed on numerous occasions by the Luftwaffe. By the end of 1944, there had been an estimated fifty-eight raids on the then relatively small town and its quiet surrounds. Woking was considered fortunate by some of its residents compared to the destruction wrought on larger cities, industrial and military centres throughout Britain. However there were prime targets that the Germans sought to destroy in the Woking area and this included the Vickers Armstrong aircraft factory at Brooklands, approximately five miles from Woking town centre. On 4 September 1940, and despite the site being camouflaged, a daytime raid by German bombers hit the factory, killing eighty-nine workers and injuring a further 419. The factory was rebuilt and returned to full scale production of aircraft as soon as possible and survived the war without being bombed again. The airfield at Brooklands was finally closed in 1982 after the British Aircraft Corporation acquired Vickers. Today little remains to indicate that this was once the area where much of the early innovations in motor racing and the aeronautical industry were developed.

High losses of bombers in daytime missions during the early years of the war from German defences, including flak and fighter aircraft, forced the RAF to switch to night time sorties. With limited effective navigational equipment at the beginning of the war, and difficulty in locating small targets at night, it was decided by military planners, and endorsed by Churchill in early 1942, that whole industrial cities would become targets by 'area bombing'. This new tactical policy occurred with the arrival of a new Commander-in-Chief of Bomber Command, Air Marshall Arthur Harris. Despite the difficulties, Bomber Command flew missions on almost every day and night of the war and continually attacked the German homeland, but not without high losses of British airmen.

Bill's induction into flight training and the experience he had often thought of since his early teen years came in 38 Squadron. Exhaustion and high stress levels caused by the knowledge that each time they took off, they might not return became a part of everyday life. The dangers were numerous on every mission: of flak (exploding shells from Anti-aircraft guns), or being shot down from enemy fighter aircraft, unfavourable weather conditions, technical problems or training accidents and enemy spotlights. Every member of crew knew that on any mission there was almost a fifty/fifty chance of not returning to base. It was not a thought Bill tried to dwell on, but it was never far from his mind. He openly admitted that, although being nervous on almost every sortie, he still derived a sense of pleasure during most flights once a mission had commenced and crews were focused on their tasks. Bill maintained this joy of flight and passion for aircraft for the rest of his life. The Wellington Bomber though was the aircraft he would spend most of his flying hours in for the duration of the war.

The Wellington 1A was the initial aircraft that Bill became acquainted with on being posted to 38 Squadron. Bill was introduced to his Flight Officer/Pilot Hopkins and the initial three flights required him to complete training, including target practice, on December 16, 20 and 29. His total flying time was a mere thirteen hours to the end of 1939. Bill was later issued with a .38 Smith and Wesson pistol, which he wore on all missions over Europe. He had a few days leave over Christmas and returned home to be with his family, where he related his recent experiences and also caught up with local news around Horsell and Woking and of course numerous discussions concerning the war at the dinner table and throughout many an evening.

Western Europe

In January 1940 Bill attended his first of the many pre-flight briefings that all crew members were put through prior to each mission. On the back wall of every Briefing Room was a half-million scale map of North West Europe. In 2004, Bill recalled that the crews were given information for their designated targets including weather conditions, wind speed and direction, flying routes and locations of known German defences such as flak attacks. Planning had to be as accurate and meticulous as possible and crews were always on the alert for attacks by German fighters. Continual vigilance was required for the total mission. Weather conditions and forecasts across selected enemy targets were paramount in determining which British air bases would be used for take-off and landing. The briefing for aircrews included details of each mission given by a Wing Commander and the Station Intelligence Officer providing target sites. Other information included engine start-up times and the runways to be used.

Then came the command; 'Get yourself crewed up.' Bill recalled collecting his parachute and 'Mae West' (aircrew life preserver in case of a landing in water) prior to each mission and changing into his flying gear in the locker rooms; all the while feeling pre-flight nerves. Before each mission, the pilot would briefly go over flight details again with his crew. When the crew was on board they waited for the signal to take off. Bill recalled that as aircraft gathered speed on the runway, most aircrews, with a full bomb and fuel load making the aircraft heavy, would hope or pray that their bomber would get off the ground safely. During one mission in June 1940, Flying Officer Hopkins, the pilot of the Wellington Bill was in, had difficulty getting airborne and then collided with an obstruction on the runway, which resulted in aborting their sortie. These situations only exacerbated crew stress levels.

There was always a danger of mid-air collisions as Bomber Command aircraft generally flew close formations on each mission and fatal accidents occurred throughout the war. These were risks and stresses that all aircrews became familiar with. Although often blinding to crews, searchlights from enemy territory could sometimes aid in locating a target. Snow, fog, drizzle, rain of varying intensities, cloud cover varying at different heights and locations, surface wind speeds and directions, runway conditions, occasionally water-logged or snowbound – all could mean having to land at an alternative aerodrome. Pilots sometimes had to fly principally by their instruments when visibility was badly reduced with inclement weather. Shell bursts from enemy defences were also a frightening experience and once the enemy target had been sighted and bombs were dropped, the crew's adrenalin remained extremely high until they were safely returned to base.

Pre-flight tasks meant ground crews, often undervalued and neglected for their essential roles to maintain aircraft, were kept busy inspecting components like internal communications systems (Intercom), instrument gauges, bomb gearing systems, arming of guns with ammunition, loading bombs and fuel and other mechanical and electrical checks of the bomber in readiness for every mission. When the crew was inside the bomber there was generally no talking at this stage. Bill recalled that when he was the Wireless Operator, he sat behind the Pilot and Co-Pilot, partly separated by a partition, and wore headgear, so very little extraneous noise could be heard from the engines. The W/O was the Liaison Officer in the bomber, handling incoming messages but only transmitting information out if there was an SOS. Approximately every fifteen minutes, the Wireless Operator would receive a coded message from Base Headquarters that could include which airfield to land at, or help with determining specific positions of their aircraft, to check that Rear gunners were not in trouble or information to assist Navigators.

Throughout the early operational months of 1940 things began to hot up. Between January 5 and 20, 38 Squadron carried out many daytime sweeps over the North Sea to sight enemy shipping. Bomb drops were carried out as required and aerial photography continued up to 20,000 ft. This period included searching for German submarines over areas near Happisburgh and coastal sweeps, sometimes with other aircraft including Whitley Bombers. Instructions from Headquarters following intelligence about possible enemy incursions occurred relatively frequently, and often six aircraft loaded with 'B' bombs were on standby.

Squadrons were also on standby for operations to attack enemy 'Flak' ships, which required aircraft to be bombed up and ready to depart at a moment's notice. Weather was also decisive in operations because levels of visibility varied with cloud cover, wind speed and direction, drizzle, rain, sleet, fog, snow, or storms. Aircraft were sometimes redirected to other bases if weather and visibility were considered precarious. Flight training for Squadrons continued between sorties and, for Bill, this included dive-bombing practice and air firing at Berners Heath in Sussex. The icing up of aircraft parts was sometimes a problem and one attempt to reduce this was to spread oil on impacted areas but this proved unsatisfactory; intense cold would even buckle some oil tanks on occasion.

High levels of stress on Air Crews were already evident at this early stage of the war with reports of sick-leave and demotion of some personnel. If thick fogs occurred which made visibility extremely difficult for flying, then aircrews were sometimes stood down. Heavy snowdrifts during January 1940 also caused 38 Squadron to be stood down and Bill recalled some crew members indulging in snow-balling and 'terraplaning' on boards towed by cars near the barracks.

Occasionally all leave would be suspended if emergencies arose like expected invasions or enemy air raids on aerodromes and other vital locations. Training exercises were carried out where feasible and, most of the time, crews remained either on standby for sorties, or were stood down until further notice. In early 1940, the Wellingtons of 38 Squadron were flown to the Vickers Armstrong factory at Weybridge to have armour fitted to their petrol tanks in preparation for what was to come.

During the early days of the war, Bomber Command flew missions over German targets with the aim of destroying part of the German naval fleet, including those based in the Heligoland Bight area of the North Sea. On 20 February, 38 Squadron took part in a night-time raid on Heligoland. The squadron set off at 11.15 pm and returned 7.45 hours later at 7am on the morning of 21 February; Bill had performed the dual role of Wireless Operator and Air Gunner. Sadly, one of the six Wellingtons on this mission, under the command of Flying Officer Hawxby, went down and the crew was never heard from again. The weather conditions experienced over the target area included cloud cover, snow and ice and pilots had to fly for much of the time by their instruments only.

The loss of Hawxby and his men, all known to Bill and fellow Wellington crew members of No. 3 Group, was just one of many tragedies for RAF Bomber Command personnel throughout the war. Crews felt the loss of their friends deeply, knowing that the next mission could also be their last. A second Wellington on this sortie ran out of fuel and crash landed approximately fifteen miles from Marham Base and, miraculously, only one crew member was injured with a fractured ankle. In 2005, Bill recalled that when personnel went for drinks after a mission, glasses were always raised for any fellow crew member killed or listed as missing. For much of his first 200 flying hours, Bill flew under the command of Flying Officer Hopkins and they became close friends. Flying Officer Hopkins was a fatherly figure, who had a reassuring, caring and courteous disposition with all crew members, but equally he could be very strict and demanding, essential attributes for combat and training.

Some crews would be on standby for 'Special Duties'. For example, on 24 February 1940, a comprehensive practice bombing program was carried out at Berners Heath. Bad weather, including rain, caused a delay in operations for several days and it was on 29 February that 38 Squadron carried out a 'nickel raid' over north west Germany, in conditions of visibility that varied from as low as 2,000 yds up to 12 miles. Thankfully, all crews returned safely home to base. 'Nickel raids' involve dropping propaganda leaflets in their millions and were considered a form of psychological warfare against one's enemies. Bill recalled that the leaflet dropping era had little perceived effect on the Germans, but the upside to this was that much valuable knowledge of German terrain was gathered. Another nickel raid and reconnaissance took place on 21 March, again over north west Germany.

Day and night time reconnaissance and sorties continued throughout March and April 1940, along with occasional nickel raids, mainly over the North Sea and north west Germany. Visibility varied from mission to mission and sometimes electrical problems could develop with an aircraft, which hampered proceedings. When sorties were being carried out, there was still the necessity of maintaining a continuous training program for crews including coastal trips, aerial photography, dive-bombing, air-firing, formation flying and searchlight co-operation. Throughout these periods most crews remained on standby for operations against the enemy.

On 9 April 1940, Bill's nineteenth birthday, information was received from Headquarters that Germany had started an invasion of Norway and some crews were immediately placed on standby notice for possible missions. On 12 April, a daytime sortie flew over the North Sea with six Wellingtons; Bill was the Wireless Operator in Wellington 9295 and during the mission, heavy fighting was encountered with German Messerschmitt ME 110s. Two Wellingtons were lost during the attack. One went down in the North Sea under Squadron Leader Nolan after a heavy engagement. The remaining aircraft had all been hit and damaged by enemy fire by the time they returned to base. All returning crews were very badly shaken up and distraught from this sortie, or 'damaged' as Bill called it. Upon returning to base, Bill said this was the first time he accepted cigarettes from ground crew; aircrews had been told that cigarettes would help calm their nerves and this resulted in his lifetime addiction to nicotine. After the heavy loss of aircraft to German fighters and anti-aircraft barrages during daytime raids, Bomber Command changed tactics and focused on night-time sorties instead and this signalled the start of Bill's problems with sleep deprivation. Despite crews exacerbated levels of exhaustion from night-time sorties, many men still found it difficult to sleep in the day after debriefing. To overcome this, crews often went out drinking - which also helped calm their nerves. Bill recalled that as the war progressed, and due to increasingly high levels of stress with each sortie, he actually saw some crew members being helped to climb up into the bombers because 'their legs were like jelly' as their physical and mental strength deteriorated.

On 16 April 1940 at 11.30 am, three Wellingtons including that piloted by Flight Lieutenant Hopkins undertook air firing, bombing practice and section drill at Berners Heath. Shortly after this, personnel were informed that at 18.10 hours, six bombers, including that of Flight Leiutenant Hopkins and his crew, were to undertake a mission to bomb Stavenger Aerodrome in a night-time raid. Bill recalled that the target was obscured by cloud and that all aircraft returned to base between 1.08 am and 1.45 am. Despite the long night and freezing conditions in the aircraft, not a single bomb had been dropped, a situation that was to reoccur on many other missions over the course of the war. Night flying operations also gave crews valuable experience in identifying enemy targets and coping with inclement weather and freezing flying conditions.

Between the hours of 9.00 pm and 2.40 am on 23–24 April, a mission to bomb Westerland Aerodrome located on the German island of Sylt off the north west coast of mainland Germany was ordered from HQ. Today, Westerland Aerodrome is used as an airport but it was significantly developed during the war and served as a military base. Sylt was used as a base for German aircraft, including the He115 Seaplane, to lay sea mines to destroy British shipping. Bomber Command was instructed to destroy the lights that were used by the Germans to aid in laying mines. The Wellington Bill was in for this sortie dropped its bomb load on the north west corner of the aerodrome and started four 'observed fires'. Glaring searchlights and intense flak fire were encountered here and Bill's aircraft suffered damage to the port engine cowling. Despite this, the six bombers and crews all returned to base safely.

Because crews had to stay awake and alert on missions that could last up to ten hours, on night-time sorties, amphetamine (Benzedrine) pills were issued to service personnel, commonly referred to as 'Wakey wakey' pills. Once safely back from a mission, and after formal reports and checks were completed, crew members ate breakfast before trying to get some well needed sleep. For many, sleeping in the daylight for more than a few hours was difficult. Bill recalled that drinking beer, spirits and wine, whether on the base or at local pubs in nearby towns and villages, was useful as a sedative between each mission and would usually provide the extra hours of sleep needed to cope with their altered body metabolism. Sleep deprivation had a gradual detrimental effect on many aircrews as the war continued. For some personnel, including Bill, sleep deprivation became the norm and would also evolve into a post-war problem. Bill's nervous system, like thousands of other Bomber Command aircrew, would also suffer from the enormous physiological and psychological pressures as a result of these missions. Fortunately, if they survived the relatively high casualty rate of Bomber Command missions, life for aircrew on returning to base also provided advantages over other armed forces personnel. They had ample cooked, nutritional and regular meals and a bed waiting for them after returning from each sortie.

In May 1940 Bill was promoted to the rank of Sergeant following a Decree from the Air Ministry which was given to all qualified and operationally flying and RAF personnel – including Wireless Operators. Throughout the months of May, June, July and up to 15 of August 1940, Bill flew at least another sixteen missions, predominantly over German targets. Bomber Command's air offensive focused on attacking industrial targets in the Ruhr including Duisberg at the junction of the River Rhine and the Ruhr Valley; Cologne, and Emden, which was a major industrial centre for shipbuilding, machinery, chemicals and cement. There were also bombing raids over Hamburg and Bremen.

May also saw the evacuation of Dunkirk, which began on the twenty-sixth. Approximately 198,000 British and 140,000 French, Belgian and Dutch troops evacuated after the German invasion of the Low Countries and Northern France. Bill recalled one particular sortie where bombs were dropped on a German convoy; he knew that many German troops would die. It was experiences like this that remained in his memory and, although upsetting, were seen as a necessity of war every time aircrews went up.

There were occasions when an operation was rescheduled due to poor flying conditions and during one sortie in June, the Wellington that Bill was in had difficulty getting airborne and hit an obstruction on the runway; their part in the sortie had to be aborted. The adrenalin of the entire crew was always high on each mission and they were thankful to have landed safely with loaded fuel tanks and a full bomb payload directly under them. Bill flew with 38 Squadron, almost entirely with Flight Lieutenant Hopkins until 15 August 1940. At the end of this Tour of Operations, he had completed 186.5 hours flying time, divided almost equally between day and night-time missions in Wellington Bombers as a Wireless Operator/Air Gunner. Bill flew his last sortie with 38 Squadron on 10 August 1940. Total Operations completed stood at twenty-six.

Chapter 3

1940: No. 20 Operational Training Unit

ollowing this tour of operations, Bill was posted on 15 August
to No. 20 Operational Training Unit at RAF Lossiemouth in
Scotland, and promoted to Instructor for newly recruited
Trainee Wireless Operators. RAF Lossiemouth was built during
1938–39 and handed over to Bomber Command in April 1940.
No. 20 Operational Training Unit was principally a training unit
for Bomber crews during the war, but some operational raids were
also launched from there although, as an Instructor, Bill was not
required to undertake any sorties.

Bill enjoyed being in Scotland again and a change of duties
provided an opportunity for his body to recover from the high stress
levels endured during his first tour of operations. Bill continued
flight training while stationed at Lossiemouth but this was done
predominantly in the Avro Anson, the only other aircraft Bill flew in
during his wartime service. The Anson was first built in 1935 to Air
Ministry specifications and became the first RAF monoplane with a
retractable undercarriage and also became the primary British and
Commonwealth Air Training plane. The Anson was developed into
a multi-engine aircraft, which was served in Coastal Command and
Search and Rescue operations. Over 11,000 Ansons were built up
to 1952, making it the second most built aircraft after the Vickers
Wellington Bomber.[8]

Apart from usual leave entitlements, Bill could not manage to
visit his family in Horsell when based at Lossiemouth because of
the long distance and the busy schedule he was committed to. He

wrote letters to his family recalling his experiences and day-to-day situations and always looked forward to receiving news from home. He still managed to indulge his love of steam trains occasionally though and one of his most treasured memories was travelling non-stop from Edinburgh to London and back again on the Flying Scotsman – which he managed at least twice. The Flying Scotsman became famous in 1934 for being the first locomotive to reach speeds of 100 mph and Bill remembered the sheer joy of travelling on this steam locomotive when it reached its maximum speed.

Bill's time as an Instructor also included a regular schedule of flying practice sorties with new recruits while facilitating an improvement with his personal proficiency. Over the fifteen months that Bill was stationed at Lossiemouth, he completed 278 separate flights. The trips were mostly over country locations on designated routes, for example to Inverness or Lakenheath and return. Some flights were used for bombing and target practice, both during the day and at night in order to train new recruits and accustom them to the rigours of flying a bomber aircraft under differing conditions. This period of Bill's service passed very quickly; there were no accidents with any flights and he remained in relatively good health. Bill's total flying time from date of enlistment to 25 November 1941 now stood at 929.30 hours.

Chapter 4

1941: No. 40 Squadron

40 Squadron – Motto: *Hostem acolo expellere* (To drive the enemy from the sky)

Badge: *A Broom.* The broom was chosen to immortalise the frequent exhortation of Major 'Mick' Mannock, the famous First World War pilot, who served with the squadron, to 'sweep the Huns (Germans) from the air!'

On 28 November 1941 Bill was posted to 40 Squadron of Bomber Command, which flew Wellington and Blenheim bombers out of two bases, Wyton and Alconbury. Bill remained with this squadron for a relatively short time until 2 February 1942, and completed six operational sorties. These raids were all done at night-time and included raids to Cherbourg, Brest, Wilhelmshaven, Hamburg, Emden and Le-Havre with each sortie ranging in duration from 3.10 hours to 6.45 hours.

There were inevitably bombing missions when targets could not be identified, especially during bad weather and cloud cover was up to '10/10'. The weather over Britain and Western Europe is subject to relatively rapid fluctuations and to overcome this unpredictability, pilots and crews sometimes had to switch priorities. This occurred when Bill flew raids over Cherbourg on 6 January and Brest on 9 January 1942 when poor weather conditions meant that the crew would return home with a full bomb load; rather than waste the sortie entirely, leaflets were dropped or, sometimes, enemy territory was photographed. On occasion, one or more bombers in a raid would skirt round a cloud covered area and try to locate the designated bomb target, and this sometimes proved successful. During the night sortie to Wilhelmshaven on 10 January 1942 the target was highly visible, but one Wellington failed to return after bombing a railway line, which was initially lit up by flares that were dropped at 12,000 ft. One Wellington went down on this raid flown by Pilot Officer Sanders and all six crew members were lost.

On the afternoon of 14 January on a bombing sortie to Hamburg, six Wellingtons were flown with relatively clear views for most of the flight to Germany, but a ground haze of mist covering the target area made a precise sighting difficult. A Wellington piloted by Pilot Officer Barr was abandoned as the heating and gyro failed and all bombs were brought back to base. Another bomber piloted by Pilot Officer Broad and his entire crew failed to return. The Wellington Bill was in skirted the coastline due to poor visibility and tried for an hour to circle the area and pin point the designated target but had to give in and return to base with its full load of eighteen 250lb bombs.

A sortie to bomb Le Havre on the evening of 31 January and morning of 1 February saw the bombs jettisoned from Bill's aircraft when it developed a mechanical failure with the aileron (the lateral control flaps at the rear of the plane's wingtips). The results of the bomb drops from the remaining Wellingtons over the target were not observed due to cloud cover. During this same sortie a serious malfunction in the port-engine of Bill's aircraft arose due to severe icing of the controls. This resulted with a complete engine cut-out ten minutes into the return flight, causing aircrew stress levels to rise further as Pilot Officer Bain had to consider the possibility of abandoning the bomber. Bill experienced first hand the capabilities of the Wellington Bomber; with only one engine operating until the stalled port-engine fortunately restarted approximately five minutes later. Pilot Officer Bain managed to return to base with all crew saved. Bill was to recall this experience later when he flew with 99 Squadron in Burma in April 1943. The Wellington he was in was one engine down and he suggested to the pilot that he keep the bomber in the air for as long as possible; the crew were ordered instead to bail out over enemy occupied territory. (See Part II)

While Bill was stationed with No. 40 Squadron, he met a fellow crew member that would become particularly close to him: Alan Thompson, who went by the nickname 'Thommo'. While off duty Bill, Thommo and other aircrew would often socialise at local pubs near the bases they were stationed at. Thommo was stationed in England throughout his service with the RAF but became a German P.O.W after having to bail out during a bombing mission. After Bill had been posted to India in June 1942, these two friends were not to meet again until after the war had finished. Following his marriage to Rene in November 1946, Bill and Thommo were reunited when Thommo visited the couple in Horsell. Thommo eventually received a job with Dutch Shell Oil Co. and lost contact with Bill after the late 1940's. The last time Bill had any communication from Thommo indicated that he had been transferred to the West Indies by this company and sadly, these two wartime friends never met again.

The antics of aircrew when socialising took many forms and Bill recalled one drink in particular, occasionally as a last order, was nicknamed the *Blue Nile* and may have originated from personnel who had returned from operations in the Middle East. The *Blue Nile* was a combination of three different spirits, a double shot of each, that was sometimes consumed as a nightcap to round off the evening. When several dozen crew members went out to a pub together, it was not unknown for the supply of beer to actually run out. Bill knew most of the crew members from the three Squadrons he was to fly in and often said after his breakdown that they were like a large family. If any crew member did not make it back to base, the empty seats or new faces at the mess table, debriefing rooms and beds in their huts became a continual reminder of the risks they all put their lives under on every mission. Crews lived together, ate meals together, flew missions together, socialised together and, in doing so, formed a strong bond of friendship, depending on each other's skills and support. By the end of January 1942 Bill had completed thirty-two operational sorties and, combined with training and instructional duties at various air bases, had accumulated a total of 973.15 flying hours.

Part II

Chapter 5

1942: No. 99 Squadron

99 Squadron – Motto: *"Quisque tenax"* (Each tenacious)

Badge: *A Puma Salient.* The Puma has a double significance: the Squadron once flew aircraft equipped with Puma engines and this animal signifies independence and tenacity of purpose.

Having been formed at Yatesbury, Wiltshire in 1917, 99 Squadron was equipped with Wellington Bombers at the start of the Second World War. Initially the Squadron was engaged in armed searches for German naval units in the North Sea, and nickel raids. By 1941 they were involved in the steady bombing of naval and industrial targets. During the early part of 1942, 99 Squadron moved to India and in November of that year began to operate against the Japanese in Burma. The main targets were enemy airfields, supply dumps and eventually railway communications. In early March of 1944, the Squadron logged its one-thousandth bombing sortie.

The Middle East: Egypt

On 5 February 1942 Bill, nearly 21 years old, received orders to transfer to 99 Squadron of Bomber Command at RAF Base Waterbeach, in Cambridgeshire, approximately 5.5 miles north of Cambridge. Throughout February and until mid-April 1942, Bill flew under the command of Squadron Leader Cook. During these first few weeks he participated in cross-country and fuel consumption tests and continued with wireless operation and air-firing practice.

At the beginning of April Bill had been selected, with several other crew members, to undertake a test trial for distance, fuel consumption, time and conditions encountered once airborne as part of the overall capability of the Wellington Bomber. The scheduled flight was from England to Gibraltar and then from Gibraltar to Cairo. Bill first had to fly from RAF Waterbeach to RAF Portreith, arriving on 12 April. Following three intense days of detailed planning and preparation that required a thorough knowledge of the flight path and technical problems that could occur with the Wellington, along with predicted weather and possible enemy attacks, the crews were passed ready for their mission.

The first leg of the flight commenced on 15 April from Portreith Air Base to Gibraltar, a distance of 1,208 miles, which took 7.40 hours flying time during daylight. The second and longest leg of this flight began on 18 April at 4.15 pm and continued into the early hours of 19 April; landing at Cairo and then onto Heliopolis to stop at Almaza Transit Camp (ATC) in Egypt. Gibraltar to Cairo for this flight path was a distance of 2,250 miles and took 12.30 hours non-stop. To do this, the squadron first flew down to West Africa and then across to the Nile. One of the crew members in the Squadron, Flight Sergeant Groocock, whom Bill had first met at Waterbeach, recalled that the Wellingtons, with the additional loaded fuel tanks built into the bombers for the flight, gave them a hair-raising moment when taking off from Gibraltar. This was because some of the bombers came within a few feet of the sea wall at the end of the runway – only just clearing it.[9]

Another concern for this flight was the suspected possibility of attacks from enemy fighters. It was rumoured that French Vichy fighters from Dakar were being paid by the Germans to attack any

British aircraft. The Vichy Government of France during the war was located primarily in the centre and south of France, based in the spa town of Vichy.[10] Officially the 'French State', Vichy France was headed by Marshall Phillippe Petain between 1940 and 1944; the creation of this Nazi approved Vichy Government was, in the minds of many French people, a betrayal by the politicians and their supporters who endorsed this agreement. The surrender of France to Germany in June 1940 was a bitter and hard-knock to French citizens who rejected this outcome. The French Vichy government also had an ally in Japan, which was considered mutually beneficial to both countries at the time. The French had ruled their colonial territories of Indo-China (today these territories are known as Vietnam, Laos and Cambodia) since the 1850s and, like their Dutch and British counterparts, the French obviously desired to retain their colonial outposts.

In *Forgotten Armies: Britain's Asian Empire & War with Japan*, Bayly and Harper write that:

When the Japanese invaded Southeast Asia in 1941-42, they preserved the rule of their French Vichy ally while clamping down hard on any sign of restiveness among the large French expatriate populations of Hanoi and Saigon, which numbered nearly 100,000. As long as pro-axis Vichy rule lasted in France the French in Saigon and Hanoi had offered little resistance to the Japanese. Even after the fall of Paris to the Allies in 1944, local French administrators collaborated fully with the Japanese, helping to put down local Chinese and communist revolts and tracking Allied Special Forces.[11]

Meanwhile Bill, under the command of Squadron Leader Cook, who was in charge of three Wellingtons and their crews, completed the trial flight to Cairo without encountering enemy fire. It was an exhausting flight, the crew had to go without sleep due to the need for the men to remain on high alert. The flight was not without tragedy however; several aircraft were lost from other groups during the night when the formation was flying over Africa on the leg to the Nile.

After reaching their destination, Bill and the rest of the crew had organised temporary accommodation in large tents situated in the desert at ATC and a relatively short distance from Cairo. This camp, used by some Allied forces stationed in the Middle East, was at the time on the edge of the desert near Heliopolis, one of the oldest cities of ancient Egypt, on the north east edge of Cairo.

Meanwhile Squadron Leader Cook and a Flying Officer Navigator headed back to England to report on their trial flight; tragically, these two crew members were never heard of again. Bill recalled that the three Wellingtons in his group under Squadron Leader Cook achieved a first in non-stop flying from Gibraltar to Cairo and again added impetus for the technical potential and durability of the Wellington Bomber and possible future developments with other types of aircraft.

In Egypt, Bill met a relatively newly experienced Co-pilot named Paul Griffiths. Bill and Paul became very close friends and spent much of their time in ATC and India training and socialising together. Bill remained at ATC for eight weeks from 19 April to 10 June 1942 until a replacement batch of Wellingtons was flown in to form a new squadron. The initial plan was that crew members would rejoin with another squadron in the Middle East and return to Britain upon completion of their tour of operations.[12]

In the interim, off-duty crew members took the opportunity to visit some of the ancient historical sights in Egypt, including the Great Pyramids of Giza, the Sphinx and the city of Cairo. There were also trips taken further north to Alexandria where personnel were able to relax, enjoy the beaches and spend time swimming in the clear coastal waters. Bill and his peers usually caught a tram that ran from their campsite into Cairo, where air crews had access to coffee houses and cafes, the Services Club in Heliopolis and local entertainment. The aircrews did not speak fluent Arabic, but they still managed to learn a number of basic words to communicate with locals and when this failed they occasionally resorted to hand signs or sketches on paper. Many crew members also visited the New Zealand Club in Cairo, one of the few places that served western food and drinks. The establishment was managed and owned by New Zealand nationals and, according to Bill, was one of the better places not only to purchase cold drinks, but to relax with other Squadron crews.

There were two Australians that Bill spent some time with at ATC: Jimmy Curr, an Air Gunner, and Bill Dickie, a Sergeant Pilot both of whom had been part of the flight from Gibraltar to Cairo. Bill got on very well with the 'Aussies' and they spent many hours together discussing numerous topics including their personal history, lifestyles and cultures of Australia and Britain, the war, families and friends and what they wanted to do with their lives if they survived hostilities. Another crew member from 99 Squadron was a Canadian Pilot nicknamed 'Newsreel Pete'. Pete was an avid photographer and took every opportunity to record on film the crews' experiences at ATC; the local Egyptian people, and the numerous historical.

The Far East: India & Burma

During this period at ATC, Bill recalled other Allied aircraft crews that regularly flew in for a stopover prior to re-engaging in their designated Tour of Operations. At the beginning of June 1942, the eagerly awaited new batch of Wellingtons arrived and available crews were redirected to fly to India. Some crew members in the camp, though they were not ordered to, also volunteered to fly some of these recently arrived bombers to India.[13] This was part of a wider campaign to bolster resources needed to fight the Japanese and its primary regional ally, the Indian National Army.

On the India–Burma front during the war, No. 99 Squadron and No. 215 Squadron stood out in operations conducted by Wellingtons when sent to the Far East. Initially based in a number of separate detachments, 99 Squadron was the first to become operational and flew into Pandaveswar on 17 June, before moving to Digri in October 1942. Both Pandaveswar and Digri are located in the West Bengal Province in the East of India; the ideal situation for No. 99 Squadron to become integrated into full operations against the Japanese.[14]

While based in India, the Wellingtons and their crews also flew stopovers to both Calcutta and Bombay (now Kolkata and Mumbai). Both cities were a culture shock to the crews. Bill remembered most of them being appalled by sights of extreme poverty of the majority of Indian locals in comparison to a very small number of wealthy people. There were two further stopovers after flying to the far north of India that provided Bill with some wonderful memories. Both sites were located at the foothills of the Himalayan Ranges of Ambala and Solan. The crew members were billeted in Ambala and it was here that they were able to visit a European styled cinema, the first since leaving England.

In both Ambala and Solan, Bill and many of the RAF personnel were able to enjoy the natural beauty of the surrounding hills, with the Himalayas in the distance on clear days when they were undertaking flight exercises. There was a train service in Solan that travelled into the local hills where the temperatures were slightly cooler. When they had a few days' leave, most crew members, including Bill, took the train to find some reprieve from the heat and to enjoy the relatively unspoilt natural scenery of the region. The train travelled at a somewhat leisurely pace on the inclines and this allowed Bill and a few other passengers to get off the carriages and walked alongside the train to stretch their legs and break the monotony of the journey.

There were very few human inhabitants in this thickly-forested area away from the town of Solan. The scenery created a great sense of solitude and peace for the crews who ventured here and the irony of these moments were not lost on crew when they considered the violence and destruction of the war being waged worldwide outside this Eden of tranquility. These days were few and far between and a war still had to be fought and won by the Allies.

Throughout the months of July and August 1942, 99 Squadron was stationed at Madras where crew members stayed at the local YMCA. During this visit, 99 Squadron held a garden party at nearby Guindy, which a number of Civic Heads and the Governor of Madras attended and were treated to a sumptuous banquet – a welcome break from the daily routine and usual fare given to RAF personnel. In India, the RAF employed Indian servants (referred to as Bearers), who were happy to earn a reasonable and consistent wage by administering to the day-to-day needs of the crews. The Bearers did all washing of clothes, cooked meals and other duties as required. Some of the meals consisted of rice and curried side dishes; food that Bill took to and developed a lifelong liking for. Eating curried food with rice as a staple was a new experience for most crew members who were used to a traditional western diet, particularly as the majority of the curried foods were very spicy.

During August and September 1942, members of 99 Squadron commenced a series of training exercises including dusk patrols, formation flying and target practice with bombs and guns. A few of these training exercises were done in co-operation with the Allied forces and the ammunition was stored at each camp. There were now nine Wellington Bombers in 99 Squadron and during October 1942, they all returned to Pandaveswar. By November, the newly reformed and trained 99 Squadron had relocated to Digri and, as well as assisting with the transport of food and supplies for Allied forces, began to operate missions against the Japanese in Burma. The main targets were enemy airfields, supply dumps, roads, railways, and river communications and 99 Squadron provided a strategic night-bombing force over Burma.

The Burma campaign was fought in the South-East Asian Theatre of the war. It was primarily a battle between British Commonwealth, American, and Chinese forces against the Empire of Japan and its main auxilliary, the Indian National Army (INA). As part of Japan's intentions to destroy Western colonial powers in South-East Asia, and in the process expand its own empire, the Japanese government set up the INA with its leader Subhas Chandra Bose, and was manned by Indian prisoners of war recruited from Japanese camps.[15] Some Indian PoWs, who by force or as volunteers, joined the INA and became guards over Allied PoWs. Bose, as Leader of the INA, and a collaborator with the Axis powers, was a vehement critic of the British, and had at one time tried to persuade the Japanese General Mutagachi that, by enlisting Indian prisoners held by the Japanese and recruited into the INA, they could mount an offensive campaign to overthrow the British Raj.[16]

In 1941 after escaping from prison in India, Bose travelled to Germany for talks with the Nazis and then returned to Japanese held Singapore. With the help of the Japanese, Bose led the 40,000 strong INA across Burma in the spring and summer of 1944 but was defeated in India. Bose also created an Indian Legion within the German Army with at least 3,000 men becoming part of the Waffen-SS in 1944. When Japan surrendered in August 1945, Bose fled India and purportedly died in a plane crash in Taiwan.[17]

This wave of nationalism across the region saw anti-colonial sentiments from other Indian dissidents like Sardar Vallabhbhai Patel within the Indian National Congress who gained further support from the INA. Many Indian civilians from Malaya, and Indian Army soldiers captured by the Japanese in Singapore in 1942, changed their allegiance to fight alongside the seemingly invincible Japanese incursion of South-East Asia and the Pacific region.[18] Anti-Colonial advocates like Gandhi who, on the surface, preached a non-violent approach to removing British rule, undoubtedly made the task of the Allied forces harder by rallying supporters to his cause as head of both the Indian National Congress and the anti-British 'Quit India' movement of 1942. It could be argued that his sentiments were nothing less than a subversive process that bolstered the agenda of Patel, Bose and their many supporters including the Japanese military.

Even President Roosevelt's Administration supported Anti-colonial sympathisers. American public opinion favoured the idea that the United States should not help to restore British territories. Roosevelt and his administration's ruminations for French Indo-China at this time may have differed depending on the intentions of the US concerning the region during and after the war. While Britain initiated a policy to relinquish some of her colonial interests after the war, France sought to retain control of its colonies in Indo-China. After the war, the US, under President Truman, adopted a policy to contain communism in the region, which was pursued more vigorously still when China became a communist state, the Peoples Republic of China, as proclaimed under Chairman Mao (Mao Zedong) on 1 October 1949.

A further issue of contention, though rarely mentioned today, on the question of America's involvement in this region by its leaders towards the end of the war and beyond is hypothesised by Seagrave in his work *Gold warriors: The covert history of Yamashita's gold*:

In 1945, American Intelligence Officers in Manila discovered that the Japanese had looted large quantities of gold bullion and other looted treasure in the Philippines. President Truman decided to recover the gold, but to keep its recovery secret. The treasure-gold, platinum, barrels of diamonds and gemstones plundered by the

Japanese military from all of East and Southeast Asia would be combined with Nazi loot recovered in Europe to create a worldwide American political action fund to fight communism.

This 'Black Gold' gave Washington virtually limitless unvouchered funds for covert operations. According to CIA officials, between 1945 and 1947 the gold bullion was secretly moved to 176 accounts at banks in 42 countries. Other treasure was recovered inside Japan during the U.S. occupation. General MacArthur, President Truman … and a handful of others, knew about the hidden plunder. Every president since Harry Truman has been involved in covering up the existence of these secret funds.

Because the treasure recovered by the United States had to be kept hidden, citizens of America and other countries were deceived. The 1951 peace treaty with Japan was distorted by these diplomatic lies, making it invalid. Because the 1951 treaty was skewed by secret deals, thousands of Japan's (war time) victims have been deprived of any compensation for their suffering.[19]

Another problem, it could be argued, that proved costly to Britain and its allies in the Second World War, was the fact that America had coerced Britain into withdrawing from a proposed naval treaty with Japan to 'limit the size of each country's naval forces in the Pacific' following World War I.'[20]

With a strong push towards an end to colonial rule by countries throughout the region, many indigenous Burmese, particularly those in central Burma and to the north, east and west, deeply resented Britain and her allies. The Japanese gained additional support from the Burmese Independence Army and, in part, by Thailand's (formerly Siam) anti-colonial supporters. In *Forgotten Voices of Burma*, Thompson argues that the indigenous Burmese of central Burma remained the greatest threat to Allied forces when it came to supporting the Japanese. For many years they had persecuted Burmese people in the hills and mountains including the Chinese.[21]

The Burmese Independence Army was established with Japanese support and one of its most revered soldiers, Aung San, had been part of the military forces that had marched into Rangoon with the Japanese in 1942. Aung San had pursued anti-colonial sentiments with a militaristic solution and, in the process, encouraged many predominantly young Burmese to take up arms against the Allies.[22] Ironically Aung San later seized an opportunity to gain independence from all colonial powers. In early 1945 the Burmese National Army, formerly the Burmese Independence Army, now led by Aung San, switched sides. They became disillusioned with the conduct of their 'new Japanese master', which had culminated in systematic looting of Burmese towns and villages as the Japanese retreated towards the end of the war.[23]

Japan's aggressive Imperialism had been apparent since the 1930s and it could be argued that all Western Allied leaders of this time were negligent to unanimously address or even thwart this overt development. Japan desired to build its own Empire and create a 'Greater East Asia Co-prosperity sphere.' The following 1936 extract, from Arthur Titherington's memoirs, himself a former Japanese PoW, highlights the intentions of Japan with regards to China.

From 1936 to 1940 are to be the test years. It is almost certain that in the early stages of this period the Military Party will attempt another coup. Political murders are likely to increase, and finally the Party will attempt to acquire complete control. Sooner or later Japan will penetrate further into China. Eventually she will overrun the whole Republic. It will mean the mightiest war the world has ever known.[24]

Japan wanted control of China's natural resources and in July 1937, war broke out between the two nations. In December, the battle for Nanking, the capital of the Republic of China, resulted in the massacre of approximately 250,000 of its citizens and revealed the nature of Japan's Imperial Army. Britain knew her colonies were at risk, and steps to prepare for the defence of Singapore, Malaya and other colonial territories proved inadequate. Japan attacked Pearl Harbour on 7 December 1941 and a day later it attacked Malaya where British ships came under fire and were destroyed. The Japanese did what the Germans had done in the early stages of the war in Europe with a 'Blitzkrieg' execution. By January 1942, Malaya had fallen. When British forces arrived in Singapore they had little air and naval support, which allowed Japanese forces to sweep across the Far East and Western Pacific Islands. Singapore fell on 15 February 1942. Lieutenant General Percival surrendered to the General Yamashita, against Churchill's request to defend at all costs. Allied leaders were shocked by the rapid advance of the Japanese over European colonies and had clearly underestimated the power of this ally to Germany and Italy. It was a humiliating defeat and again, Allied leaders from all nations should share some of the blame for this outcome.

Winston Churchill responded to Japan's aggression by planning to send men and equipment from the Middle East, even before the unexpected fall of Malaya and Singapore. This included British ships, RAF Squadrons and Allied army Divisions, two of which were the 6th and 7th Australian. A long held myth by many, not just in Australia, was that the Australian Labor Party Prime Minister of this time, John Curtin, 'brought the 6th and 7th Divisions back.' This is untrue. Churchill made the decision to channel resources to the Far East and Western-Pacific. Stanley states that Japan had in fact decided not to invade Australia because it was too heavily committed to battles in other parts of Asia, including China. Churchill and

William Tate (Bill's father) during the
First World War.

Bill's mother and father in December 1918.

Bill's father William Tate, back row, second left. He is pictured here with his Regiment on the Western Front during the First World War, during which he served with the 8th Yorkshire Regiment of 'The Green Howards'.

Horsell Primary School, attended by Bill, Bob, Ivy, Esther and Irene.

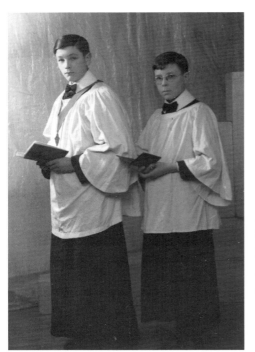

Bill and Bob as choir and altar boys in 1935, at St Mary's Church in Horsell (Church of England) and the Tate family's House of Worship.

Roosevelt in time both criticised Curtin for his apparent lack of judgement. Stanley further argues that 'Curtin's flawed leadership with his decision to allow America's General Douglas MacArthur's dominance, between March 1942 and September 1944, approaches an abrogation of responsibility.'[25]

In March 1942, General MacArthur took control of the war effort in the Pacific and became Supreme Allied Commander. He was expected to stop the Japanese advance in this region and lead the counter-offensive. The Japanese needed to control Burma and wanted to close the Burma Road, a vital route in supplying the Chinese in their war against Japan. Capturing Burma was of course the precursor to invading India, which Japan sought to exploit for its natural resources. At this stage, the Japanese possessed a superior air and naval force, and their soldiers had proven skills in jungle warfare.[26]

By May 1942, the Allies had retreated from Burma, accompanied by mainly refugees, predominantly Indian and Anglo-Burmese. The Japanese push towards India had been halted on the Chindwin River because of the heavy monsoon rains, which created impassable conditions on the roads and tracks through the mountainous frontier between India and Burma. The Allies had to reorganise, plan and build a fighting force to stop, or at least minimise, the Japanese advance then go on the offensive to retake Burma when the worst of the annual monsoon had abated.[27] No. 99 Squadron was part of this redeployment of men and equipment from the Middle East to the Far East and Pacific war zones. Conditions in the Far East were very different from those that Allied forces had experienced in Europe and the Middle East. Unlike the Japanese, the allies were not initially prepared for jungle warfare. The monsoon season meant that effective fighting against the enemy might only be possible for approximately five to six months of a year and made the Burma

Campaign a long-drawn out conflict. By early 1942 the Japanese, with support from its allies, had conquered Burma.

Geographically, Burma is slightly smaller in size than the US state of Texas. Around two thirds of the country is mountainous, and during the war, the hill country was covered with thick jungle, and had been described by some aircrew during as 'like looking into a bed of parsley' from the air.[28] The temperatures are generally hot and humid with a five-month monsoon season that can bring cyclonic winds, violent electrical thunderstorms and turbulence, which makes flying a highly risky option and could even destroy aircraft in mid-flight. The heavy rains associated with this weather, along with the damp heat, increased the risk of malaria, dengue, dysentery and jaundice. Members of the Allied armies recorded temperatures as high as 105 degrees with ninety-five per cent humidity while crossing gradients up to 45 degrees during the Burma Campaign. This was in addition to the ever-present leeches and numerous other biting insects, especially mosquitoes. One of the worst infections to get was a 'naga' sore, which spread rapidly across the body. Tens of thousands of men in the Allied armies were afflicted with many of these illnesses during the longest land campaign fought by Western Allies in the war against the Japanese and their allies.

Bill had been promoted to Flight Sergeant in December 1942. He flew in Wellington 'P' throughout 99 Squadron missions over Burma with Flight Lieutenant MacDonald as Pilot and Sergeant Paul Griffiths as Co-Pilot. The primary aim of these sorties was to halt the Japanese advance into India and China. Between 18 November 1942 and 29 March 1943, many sorties and bombing raids were carried out on targets such as Meiktila Aerodrome and roads, Sagaing railway lines and jetty, Lanywa (first aborted due to severe weather conditions), He Ho Aerodrome and surrounding targets, parts of Mandalay including railway lines, engine sheds and junctions, Bume in Akyab, Thazi (railway junction) and Toungoo

The former Woking County Grammar that Bill and his younger brother Bob attended in the 1930s.

The teenage Tate children. Left to right; Bill, Bob, Ivy, Irene and Esther.

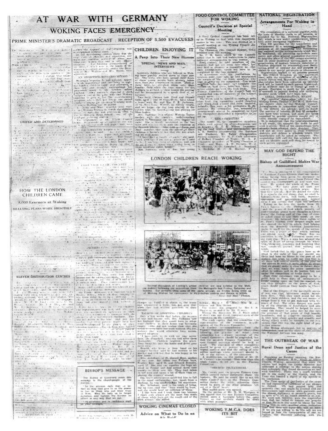

Notice of the outbreak of war in the *Woking News and Mail* and a selection of advertisements during 1938/9 informing local residents of necessary precautions and essential equipment deemed appropriate for their protection.

The new recruits; Bill (The Royal Air Force) and Bob (The Royal Corps of Signals).

Arthur Cox (Military Police) during the First World War.

John Cook (Royal Artillery) during the Second World War.

Ronald Cox (British Army) during the Second World War.

Reginald Cox (British Army & M.P.) during the Second World War.

The Wellington Bomber.

Bill (Wireless Operator and Air Gunner) second left and (Flying Officer) Hopkins, second from right, going over mission details with fellow crew members of 38 Squadron prior to their sortie. Their designated Wellington Bomber is behind the crew at RAF Base Marham in Norfolk, 1940.

Bill and Norman Russell, 38 Squadron (1940).

Wellington Bombers in flight.

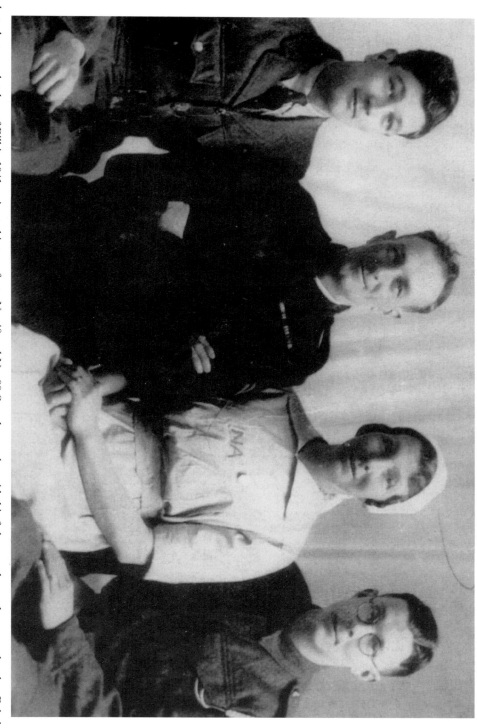

The last photograph taken of Bill in 1941, prior to his transfer to No. 40 and No. 99 Squadrons, alongside his father, mother and younger brother Bob, left to right; Bill (Royal Air Force), William (Air Raid Precautions), Elizabeth (Nursing Auxiliary Service), and Bob (Royal Corps of Signals).

The Middle East: Almaza Transit Camp (ATC) near Cairo, 1942.

Bill at the Almaza Transit Camp in 1942.

Street scene in Cairo, taken from the New Zealand Club, 1942.

Two Australians from 99 Squadron, Jimmy Curr and Bill Dickie, 1942.

Alexandria, Egypt. Jimmy Curr, Bill and Bill Dickie enjoying a day at the beach.

Egyptian water well, 1942.

A funeral procession in Cairo, 1942.

Jim Goad and Bill Dickie at the Pyramids of Giza, 1942.

The Services Club, Heliopolis, 1942.

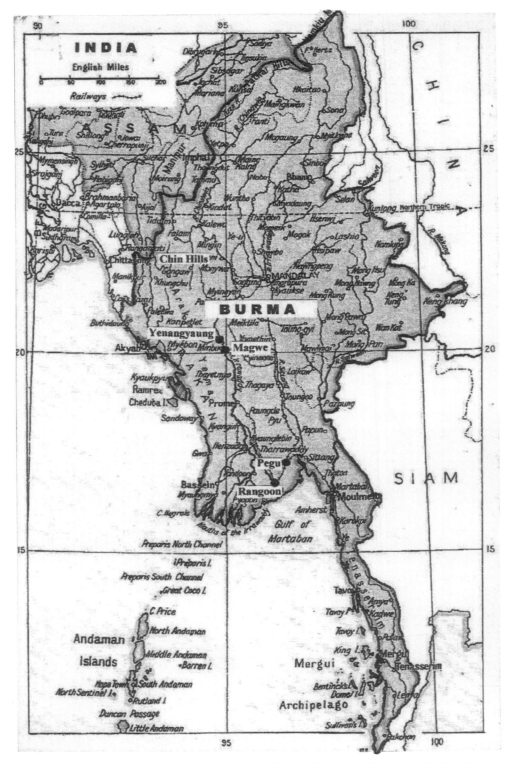

Burma (now Myanmar) and surrounding countries of India, China and Siam (now Thailand) during the Second World War.

Flight Lieutenant McDonald, 1942.

Jeff Ely, Navigator, 1942.

The train journey from Pandaveswar to Madras took five days. RAF personnel at a station stop en route at Secunderabad. Here, they are seated with an Indian Officer.

The Connemara Hotel in Madras, frequented by 99 Squadron when on leave.

A garden party for 99 Squadron with the Governor of Madras and local Civic Heads in attendance, at Guindy, near Madras, 1942.

Aerodrome. Not one Wellington from 99 Squadron was lost at this point by March 1943 although there were a few recorded incidents of attacks from Japanese enemy fighter planes and occasional flak bursts during their sorties. Depending on the targets for each sortie, the major operations took place predominantly at night-time and flying duration ranged from 6.55 hours to 9.35 hours. Bill continued to fly as the Wireless Operator/Air Gunner for most missions; his Tour of Operations was nearing its completion and his total flying time to 29 April 1943 was 1,256 hours.

Bailing Out

At 1.20 pm on 1 April 1943, Bill took off from Digri on his fifty-first operational sortie. The target was the town of He Ho and the goal was to attack dispersal pens situated slightly south east of central Burma in the state of Shan. Several of these Wellingtons and their crews had made this flight before to bomb He Ho Aerodrome. Based on an earlier mission to He Ho, the sortie should have taken between approximately eight and ten hours in total, depending on factors such as wind direction and speed. The bombers had full fuel and bomb loads; no Japanese fighter planes were encountered, nor any anti-aircraft shells or flak.

About eight hours into the mission, and probably not less than 150-200 miles from the Indian border (according to first reports) the aircraft were confronted with 'intense darkness and bad weather'. An engine cut out on 'P' Wellington, the aircraft aboard which Bill was acting as Wireless Operator. Flight Lieutenant MacDonald and second Pilot Sergeant Paul Griffiths desperately tried to restart the engine. The turbulence was strong and buffeting the plane so Flight Lieutenant MacDonald contacted base and reported that the crew would have to abandon the aircraft, then gave orders to all men to bail out. Flight Lieutenant MacDonald told his crew that he hoped they would all be safe, and instructed them to try and make their way back to India, either as a group or by themselves if necessary. The crew also knew the Japanese were in control of Burma and by this stage of the war, many of the Burmese Bamar population supported Japanese forces.

While the crew began to parachute out, Bill had a flash back and recalled a similar situation on a sortie with No. 40 Squadron. The bomber at that time was a Wellington being flown by Pilot Officer Bain; a stalled engine had been eventually restarted after approximately five minutes of losing power. Bill immediately recounted this experience to Flight Lieutenant MacDonald and asked if he could try to keep the bomber airborne for a bit longer in the hope that the disabled engine would restart. With the seconds counting, Flight Lieutenant MacDonald stood by his decision to abandon the aircraft, and Bill was the second last crew member to bail out, swiftly followed by Flight Lieutenant MacDonald. This issue remained contentious between Bill and his Flight Lieutenant; Bill maintained throughout his post war years that the pilot's judgement was questionable on this occasion. The signal sent by Flight Lieutenant MacDonald was recorded at approximately 11.00 pm, and the area was given as *'Chin Hills in enemy occupied territory'*. Chin Hills (now Chin State) is a mountainous region of North West Burma with elevations ranging from 5,000 to 9,000 ft. The recorded population of this area in 1941 was around 186,000. There were small farms in this region that grew mostly rice and millet, but with Japanese forces located here, and some locals being supportive of the Japanese, the outlook was not considered very favourable for any Allied serviceman if captured.

In the few seconds before bailing out, and with his adrenalin rising dramatically, Bill quickly checked his Irvin parachute. His mind was splintered with numerous thoughts and emotions, but Bill tried to focus on making it safely to the ground. This was the first time he had ever had to abandon an aircraft – and so near to the end of a

Tour of Operations. Bill also understood that luck had, up to this point, been on his side. All he could do now was rely on his Irvin parachute, the principal parachute used by the RAF employing the 'rip-cord' system. The design and reliability of the Irvin parachute meant it saved the lives of many thousands of Allied servicemen throughout the war. All airmen who were saved by using the Irvin parachute were automatically accepted into the 'Caterpillar Club', formed exclusively in 1922 for such veterans.

All six members of 'P' Wellington's crew successfully bailed out, but the actual location was in fact central Burma, which Bill had initially believed to be the case, and not Chin Hills. Bill surmised on occasions that the false information was delivered to possibly confuse the enemy. At the time of bailing out, Bill could not see anything immediately either below or around him in the pitch-black surroundings as his eyesight adjusted to the darkness. Hoping for a safe landing, Bill realised that he had not had time to collect his ration pack. Within a few minutes of bailing out of the Wellington, he landed in a relatively well-cleared field which suggested there were almost certainly villages nearby. The only consolation was that he had landed in the only bush in the field, which helped to cushion his fall; because of his flying gear, he was more or less unscathed apart from some scratches and bruises. Bill's mind now focused on how to make his way out of Burma and hopefully reunite with the rest of his crew. He knew the general geographical layout of Burma from the pre-flight procedures for each mission, and knew there would be villages nearby. After removing and covering his parachute he tried to gather his thoughts and remain calm. All Bill could hear in the oppressive darkness and near silence was the occasional noise of insects. He called out a few times thinking some of his fellow crew would hear but with no response.

For the time being Bill decided to head in a north-west direction, assuming that there would be a river and water supplies used by the local villagers. Because many Burmese were actively supporting the Japanese, Bill decided to avoid entering any village if he found himself in sight of one. Some of the vegetation was jungle growth, which hampered his movement, but there were occasional clearings. He was unable to sleep and so many thoughts raced through his mind: how to survive in this terrain without being taken prisoner; what his family were doing and would he ever see them again? With no ration pack and his water bottle almost empty, he desperately needed to find both food and water to stay alive. He was also only seven days away from his twenty-second birthday and wondered now, the first of many more times, how long he would survive. The air was warm so Bill removed most of his flying gear but kept his battle dress jacket with him; despite being exhausted and having had no sleep for nearly twenty-four hours, Bill walked throughout the night.

As dawn broke on 2 April, the temperature rose markedly and by mid-morning, Bill's thirst and lack of fluids were taking a toll on his body. He had not located any water and it was uncomfortably hot, even in the shade of some trees. Bill had already stripped to his shirt and trousers but kept his flying boots on to avoid cutting himself. Bill realised, with his increasingly exhausted condition, that he was becoming dehydrated and it wasn't long before he began to hallucinate. He recalled that by nightfall, and almost twenty-four hours after bailing out, his 'tongue was now very swollen, painful and extremely dry. I had no other option than to drink my own urine to stay alive.' There had been no rainfall since he had landed, but some thick, menacing clouds had been building up on the horizon and what sounded like thunder rumbling in the distance. The monsoon season was looming and Bill recalled wishing for an early. Bill sat down under the cover of vegetation and tried chewing some leaves for moisture to ease the dryness of his mouth and throat, but this was a bitter tasting experience.

He fell asleep from exhaustion for a couple of hours, but by early morning of 3 April was extremely weak. Becoming unstable on his feet, he took to crawling for short distances. Finding himself on a low incline, he noticed a muddied water hole beside a dirt track at the bottom. He partly slid and partly rolled down to the edge of the water hole and passed small handfuls of water into his mouth to satiate his thirst before pouring water over his body. He lay on the ground, trying to regain some energy and hydrate himself; filling his water bottle, he kept drinking small quantities of water. In 1995, Bill said: 'I had never experienced such thirst, dehydration and hallucinations and felt I would not have survived much longer.'

He had been at the water hole for around fifteen to twenty minutes when he noticed some Burmese women approaching with containers obviously used to collect water. The village women saw Bill but did not approach him; speaking in their own dialect, they quickly departed back from the direction they had come. Realising that he could be in danger and did not have his RAF issued Smith & Wesson with which to defend himself, Bill immediately crawled back up the bank and hid amongst some bushes. A short while later, a group of five Burmese men armed with Kukri knives appeared, spotted Bill in the bushes, and surrounded him. Bill was still extremely weak and had to be assisted to his feet. The five Burmese men helped him into their nearby village. Bill had no understanding of their language and when he arrived in the village, he was placed inside a bamboo and wood constructed hut and fed, as he recalled: 'a wonderful meal of rice and tomatoes' and tea to drink. He slept all day on a bamboo mat and was woken at dusk by one of the village men who understood a few words of English. Bill asked this villager if he would take him towards the coast near Akyab, which was approximately 170 miles due south.

The Burmese villager agreed to help so, on the morning of 4 April, after eating a breakfast of rice with some type of mashed vegetable, Bill was placed in the back of a cart drawn by a bullock. He knew that Burma was under Japanese control, but had to make a decision and take his chances. Feeling slightly rested and more alert after his ordeal, Bill hoped that travelling to Akyab would be a good way to get out of Burma without having to confront Japanese forces in one of their outposts. The only other real option was to travel through across Burma towards India, but the imminent onset of early monsoon showers would have made this journey extremely arduous and, he surmised, doomed to failure.

Life for the Tate Family in Horsell

Meanwhile back in Great Britain, the Tate family faced extremes of worry and some joy, hardship and some comfort, gains and some losses, moments of frustration and some laughter but, above all else, there remained the simple acceptance of making their contribution towards the war effort and supporting one another. The Tate family did what thousands of other citizens throughout Britain were also doing: they billeted an evacuee from Holland. When the war started, plans were implemented alone to evacuate around four million children, mothers, and pregnant women from major cities into rural areas. Some evacuees returned to their homes during the war, but evacuations were instigated again with the commencement of the Blitz on British cities on 7 September 1940, which continued unabated until May 1941. The 7 September became known as 'Black Saturday'. As war raged, life for British citizens carried on as normally as was possible. William and Elizabeth, both in their early forties at the outbreak of hostilities, had lived through the First World War and the Great Depression, and retained vivid memories of the loss, destruction and misery that so many people of their generation experienced. William had fought on the Western Front as part of the 8th Yorkshire Regiment (The Green Howards) for the entire war and suffered several combat wounds, the most serious of which occurred when a bullet passed through his right shoulder. There were several wounds to his legs and other parts of his body, most likely from shrapnel barrages and the death and carnage he had witnessed would remain with him for the rest of his life.

William and Elizabeth were aware that both their sons could lose their lives during the Second World War. In response to the call for volunteers in the war effort by King George, the Prime Minister, and military, William joined the ARP (Air Raid Precautions). Elizabeth volunteered to become part of the Nursing Auxilliary Service and worked in the Victoria Cottage Hospital in Woking. With a drastic shortage of resources when hostilities commenced, the British government requisitioned the Tate's car. Sacrifices like these were not unusual as the British economy was re-organised to build the armaments and vital war supplies required by the armed forces and for the defence of the nation and its people.

When Bill and his younger brother Bob were both away on duty, Elizabeth would sometimes sing along to the national anthem of 'God save the King' when it was broadcast. Elizabeth, however, rearranged some of the words and her rendition of the anthem went something like this:

> God save our Bill and Bob
> Long live our Bill and Bob
> God save them both
> Allies victorious
> Happy and glorious
> Long to come home to us
> God save our sons.

Then, on 2 April 1943, nearly two weeks after the crew to which Bill belonged was listed as missing, the news that Elizabeth and William had always dreaded arrived at their front door. The Letter of Advice to Next of Kin stated that Bill had been reported as 'Missing' after a bombing sortie over central Burma. The news was devastating. Very little information was given surrounding the details because nothing else was known. It would be two long and tormented years before the Tate family received word of Bill's circumstances following the Allied forces liberation of Burma. When the letter of Bill's disappearance had been read through several times, the rest of the family and relatives were informed as soon as possible. Bill's younger brother Bob was home at this time.

With Elizabeth and William trying to come to terms with this news, their eldest daughter Ivy recalled seeing Bill's younger sibling Bob crying in the back yard, thinking he may never see his only brother and close confidante again. With the loss of so many young men, spiritualism became popular in Britain for those hoping to make contact with a loved one. As the months passed by without further information from the war office, Elizabeth, desperate for any news about Bill, would sometimes visit a Spiritualist; a local woman in Horsell village, in an attempt to cope.

1943: Incarceration; 'Delivered unto Nippon'

Treatment by Japanese forces of their Prisoners of War and thousands of civilians throughout their incursions into newly invaded territories were abominable. If we had not ourselves survived many of these experiences, of having undergone such ferocity of suffering and torture, many of the reports, of which large numbers were eventually destroyed by Nippon, both during the final months and after the war had ended, might have, in the course of historical documentation, been dismissed as fallacies of our minds. But they were true and we occasionally received information in Rangoon by newly arriving prisoners of atrocities committed elsewhere by our enemy.

First Contact – The memoir of William Tate

I dozed off soon after leaving the village and was laying down in the back of the bullock cart when I was roused by raucous voices shouting at me. I was surrounded by a group of Japanese soldiers, with rifles and fixed bayonets pointed at me, and yelling; predominantly in Japanese, but also 'out' in English. They were indicating for me to climb down from the cart. This was my initial encounter with Japanese soldiers and one of the first things I noticed about my adversary was how short they were in stature compared to most Westerners. Whether the Burmese villager leading the bullock cart had intentionally taken me to these Nip soldiers I would never know, but in my mind I have always suspected this was the case. I know for a certainty that the Japanese were paying many Burmese nationals to do so.

I was searched for documents and firearms but I had no items on me that would provide any information. Any documents that could assist the enemy were, by orders from our superiors, not to be kept in our possession. If we were forced to bail out, any documents held by crews usually needed to be destroyed or buried. Under armed escort, I was taken in the back of a bullock cart to some Japanese outpost, which I was later informed was south of Yenangyaung. No attempt at communication passed between the Japanese soldiers and myself. They chatted away to each other and only offered me a small amount of water to drink.

Arriving at this location I was able to have a wash of sorts and was then given a small bowl of plain rice to eat and some tea. I was placed in a hut for the night and two armed guards promptly stood watch over me. I slept fitfully for short periods and, on the morning of April 5, was given more rice and tea. From here I was taken a short distance to what appeared to be a Japanese training camp and placed inside a bamboo cage, barely high enough to sit up straight. In extremely high temperatures, I was imprisoned like some wild animal and, throughout most of the day, a number of Japanese soldiers approached the cage, prodding me with their weapons and bamboo poles or occasionally pinching my body as if to see what my reaction would be. I could do nothing to respond, at least not in the manner I wanted to respond, and endeavoured to hide my anger and discomfort at this treatment. The only other food and fluids provided during the day was more rice with a few vegetables and tea during the afternoon.

By late afternoon and in hot and humid conditions, I was released from my 'cage' and escorted to the officer in charge who sat on a raised section of bamboo floor. No names were given to me and I possessed no knowledge of the Japanese language. Without warning I was suddenly beaten several times by two armed guards using their rifle butts on my arms and upper body. In broken English one guard yelled at me: 'take off boots…', which I promptly obeyed. I then sat down in front of the officer and again, without any indication, was hit by a guard with two hefty slaps on my face. The officer then spoke to me in relatively good English, and in an officious and arrogant tone said: 'You did not bow to me.' I then bowed for the first time to this officer. He removed his military sword from its scabbard and told me: 'I cut two Englishmen in half at Singapore with this sword.' As if to intimate he would have no compunction in killing me at will as he held the weapon in front of my face. Reports had reached Allied headquarters of Japanese soldiers beheading and bayoneting thousands of prisoners and civilians, among other atrocities, and this possible fate might yet be mine.

I moved my body slightly and moved one arm to rub part of my knee, now in some pain from an earlier injury. I then reached out to touch this officer's sword in front of me and was hit violently on the side of my face by a guard, which indicated to me I could not move without being authorised by the officer. For some reason, I thought I would test the will of my interrogator, as I had not yet provided any information considered to be of use to him. The officer said that no one other than himself would ever touch his 'sacred' sword without permission. Further personal details were asked of me, including the names of my mother and father. Any questions concerning my mission details, the number of aircraft we had and so on, I replied to only by conceding my name, rank and service number which he duly noted down. When this interrogation was terminated, almost immediately my hands were tied behind my back as the officer gave orders to the guards. One of the two armed guards held the end of the rope and, with the second guard nearby, proceeded to walk me round the camp to show the new Japanese recruits, some of whom had never seen a white Western man before. I was then taken to a private's room and 'dumped' in a corner for the night. The new guards on duty never left me once and escorted me to and from the latrine when I needed to use it. I had another very stressful night while catching a few broken hours of sleep.

By the early light of the morning of April 6 I was in considerable pain from the beatings I had received the previous day, with several large contusions now appearing on my body. My jaw was slightly stiff when I tried to move it and felt partly swollen. I had more rice and tea for breakfast, which I just managed to keep down. Without any explanation, I was placed into the back of a bullock cart again. This was done with armed guards watching over me the entire time, and I was transported a relatively short distance to another Japanese military facility, apparently near Magwe. The river on which Magwe is located is the Irrawaddy. As far as I could tell, I had been travelling in a predominantly southerly direction from my point of capture; I had been making observations of the geography and noting the direction of the suns movement. Upon arrival at this outpost I was interrogated by the senior officer where once again I gave only my name, rank and service number. There were two attempts by this officer to obtain information from me. I refused to answer any questions detailing the intention of the mission, other squadron resources and numbers of personnel at our base prior to bailing out of the Wellington, and kept silent about military operations by the Allied forces. The officer sat stony-faced in front of me and then called three guards outside his quarters to enter. I was taken outside to a nearby tree where one of the three guards tied my hands and, with the longer piece of rope free, threw this over a branch. Two guards then hauled me up so I was lifted off the ground and left hanging by my wrists. This form of torture is sometimes referred to as 'Suspension', and the end result for many PoWs would be to have their shoulder joints removed from their sockets. The pain on my wrists and shoulder blades was excruciating. I tried to lift my legs as close to my chest as possible to alleviate the strain on my upper body. One of the guards commenced beating my back with the butt of his rifle, while a second guard with a short pole, possibly bamboo, started striking my chest and abdomen. I cannot recall the number of times I was hit until I yelled: 'I talk.' As the guard in front moved to release me, the guard behind me grabbed both my legs and held them as my upper body fell forward. I landed heavily on the ground with the upper half of my body taking the brunt of the impact. To this day I wonder how my body did not suffer breaks to any bones or dislocations.

I was returned to the officer for further interrogation and I concocted a lie about my flight details, which he seemed to accept as a plausible explanation. The officer recorded parts of this information prior to my being placed under armed guard for the night. Again, the meal provided for me was boiled rice and tea. The following morning, April 7, and still in much discomfort from earlier punishment, I was led by the same officer who had sought information from me the previous day. On this occasion, six armed soldiers attended the officer as we walked to what appeared to be a parade ground which had a small boxing or wrestling ring at one end. There I was told to remove my battledress jacket and to stand in front of the ring. Having done this, the officer lined up the six armed soldiers and ordered them to raise and aim their rifles at me.

I stood stiffly to attention ... fearing the worst, and tried to control my emotions despite my adrenalin charged state. I attempted to breathe deeply as sweat accumulated on my face and body, and recall my heart thumping in my chest as well as feeling nauseous. I focused on thoughts of my mother and family and waited in dread for my execution. For some reason I noticed out of the corner of my eyes that the officer had not removed the sword from his scabbard, whereupon he immediately ordered arms down and the soldiers walked away. The officer approached me and sharply said: 'If you had asked for mercy I would have had you shot.' It is hard to explain to someone the emotional impact of this experience; going from absolute fear to some momentary trance of relief and then back again into a state of panic. Put simply, my life was still on a knife-edge. The officer then had me follow him into his quarters and offered me several brown sugar balls to eat. The sweet taste of these was wonderful after the past few days from eating mostly small quantities of boiled white rice. The officer, who never gave his name, then became quite affable and talkative having said that he had also been in India at one stage for some length of time. The notable alteration in his attitude towards me was somewhat capricious and disconcerting, given my punishment to date. He then informed me that I was to be transferred to a prison camp in Rangoon, but gave no other details of what I could expect. Throughout these days of initial capture, I managed to get only a few hours sleep so I was almost always in an exhausted state.

On the day of departure, a guard came and retied my hands prior to my being placed in the back of a lorry, which then conveyed me to Rangoon (now Yangon and former capital of Burma until 2005), which is situated on a coastal peninsula in lower Burma at the convergence of the Yangon and Bago Rivers. Rangoon has a tropical monsoon climate with an average annual high temperature of approximately ninety degrees Fahrenheit and an average low of seventy-three degrees. The average humidity is approximately seventy-four per cent, and average yearly rainfall is greater than 100 inches over 130 days. The monsoon weather and seemingly interminable heavy downpours of rain during a five to six month season strikes with ferocity between May and October.

I noticed a few things upon my arrival in this city, and most obvious was the famous golden domed Schwedagon Pagoda, which still remains today and is a major site of worship for the Burmese people and other pilgrims. By this time I was very tired, with pain in several parts of my body from the earlier beatings, and cramps, which were exacerbated by sitting in one position on the floor of the truck for many hours. As I looked out the back of the truck, I saw a tree-lined street that I would become familiar with over the next two years. This was Commissioner Road; from here it was straight towards my new abode.

Solitary confinement and torture

I was now inside Rangoon Gaol. At this time, the gaol was an Ex-British surrounded by a 25 ft high brick wall. In time, most prisoners would memorise the prison layout, which consisted predominantly of seven rectangular, two storied buildings (Blocks) of a dismal appearance. These radiated out, like spokes on a bike wheel, from a central water tower and were separated by wire fencing. No communication was allowed between PoWs with those in another compound or they would be immediately punished if caught. But we found ways of communicating, including sign language and outside contacts during work parties. In each block of a compound there was a latrine, a trough of water, and cooking facilities. Sentries could walk around the central water tower and observe each radiating block that held the prisoners.

When the gates were shut I had a quick glance at my immediate surroundings and noticed several other PoWs walking about a compound, some of whom looked at me so I nodded my head slightly in acknowledgment as I dared not attempt to speak to anyone for fear of being noticed and beaten by a Nip guard. Prisoners were almost entirely of four nationalities, I was eventually informed; mostly British, American, Chinese and Indian but also a few Australian, Ghurkas, New Zealanders, Canadian and Dutch. About half of the PoWs were white Westerners. The majority of prisoners of each nationality were kept in separate blocks and I believe that this was to assist the Japanese authorities with their administrative procedures and their particular dislikes for one nationality over another. Three blocks were occupied by British, Americans, Australian, New Zealand and Dutch PoWs; two by Indians (and Ghurkas), and one by the Chinese.

The statistics detailing survival rates are indicative of the appalling treatment of prisoners in Rangoon. More than thirty per cent of all prisoners captured in 1942 died. This casualty rate was typical of other Allied PoWs captured by the Japanese but a stark contrast to the death rate of four per cent of British and American PoWs in Europe. Most of the lives of Japanese PoWs hands could have been saved had there been adequate medical facilities, medicines, proper hygiene and sufficient nutritional food. In Rangoon, as far as I knew, there were approximately 12-1500 prisoners held here at any one time during my period of incarceration. Indian prisoners who refused to join the Japanese in their cause also suffered brutal punishment. On many occasions Indian PoWs would, when possible through their prison channels, pass food, tobacco and other much needed and sought items to men in other compounds.

[EDITOR]

It was known that captured Allied airmen were punished more severely than many other PoWs by Japanese forces. Allied aircrews were sometimes designated as 'Criminal Prisoners' and not Prisoners of War. Every captured airman spent time in solitary confinement. Although all prisoners in Rangoon were subject to horrific punishment, a captured Australian pilot named Lionel Hudson was told by one RAF pilot that: 'We're the bleeding villains, the whipping post', Hudson argues that the reason that Allied aircrew were treated with a heightened degree of animosity was initially viewed as a response to heavy bombing over Rangoon in November 1943, when Burmese civilians were allegedly killed. The truth of the matter was that, by this time, Allied air forces had gained supremacy of air space over Burma and were also bombing mainland Japanese targets. This frustrated Japan's war plans to such an extent that severe personal retribution was enacted ever more violently towards captured air force PoWs.[29]

In *Return Via Rangoon*, Stibbe writes that the Japs demonstrated a greater antipathy towards American airmen. Many of these men, if they found themselves in Rangoon, would be first sent to what was called the *Military Police Gaol*. Some of the reports of treatment to these prisoners were horrific and an untold number of Allied personnel never survived.[30] Hudson stated that, of fifty-seven airmen sent here in the first six months, following an edict by the Burma Area High Command from November 1943 regarding treatment to captured Allied airmen, at least twenty-three died from disease and beatings.[31]

Such antagonism and cruelty towards an American aircrew comes from the following extract;

The six man crew of an American bomber shot down near Rangoon was brought into the solitary cells of No. 5 Block. With one exception they were all badly burnt. For several days they were left by the Japs with their wounds undressed. When our medics were allowed to treat their burns, it was too late. In some cases their faces and other parts of their bodies were a mass of maggots. With the one exception they all died screaming in agony as they had done since their arrival. The Japs supplied no painkillers. We could hear their screams at night and even more so during the day as we worked in the garden below the solitary block.[32]

Severe ill-treatment occurred to captured Allied Airmen wherever the Japanese forces happened to be. Slattery recalled the punishment given to a captured New Zealand pilot, Norman Vickers, in the Pacific war zone.

Vickers had been shot down over the Bougainville area in the Solomons. Landing safely, he was hunted and eventually captured by the Japanese. After beatings and torture he was shipped to Rabaul in New Britain. Vickers came in for long sessions of torture such as airmen faced when Japanese tried to make them tell of squadron strengths, admit the bombing of civilian populations and so on. But one torture which was applied to the R.N.Z.A.F. man seems unique in the annals of Japanese ferocity. It consisted of binding the prisoner tightly with ropes in which fish-hooks were fastened at intervals. The ropes were twisted about the victim's head in such a way that the slightest movement or struggle from cramp tore the barbed hooks into his face. Norman Vickers died in 1944 at Rabaul from the effects of ill-treatment, dysentery and malnutrition.[33]

Once inside the walls of the prison my hands were untied and my name and rank checked. I was issued with a card detailing my Prisoner Number: 59. Without delay I was escorted by armed guards to Block 5, where I was placed into solitary confinement in Cell 2. For many air force personnel, this treatment went on for months or sometimes years. The only time some PoWs in this Block saw sunlight was when they had to empty latrine boxes, were allowed outside the building, or sent out on work parties. Most of Compound 5 was filled with aircrew from the end of 1943 until liberation.

I remained in this concrete 'hole' of a cell for one month without communicating to any other prisoner. Absolute silence was enforced by the guards, and we were immediately punished if caught trying to speak to other prisoners. The interior of this block was somewhat dim with the walls covered in a dirty, unpleasant looking whitewashed paint. There was no water for washing and by the end of this confinement, my skin was covered in a layer of grime and body sweat, from which I could observe a slight discolouration of my skin when exposed to the daylight. My clothes gradually became equally filthy from accumulated days of squalor. I also had a newly developing beard due to a lack of any shaving material. The air was usually humid, stifling and stale given the near non-existence of any ventilation. There were numerous insects including mosquitoes and flies in the cell at all times and, being of such prolific numbers, further augmented my misery. I would wake up with mosquito, bed bug or lice bites on my body; the lice made my skin itch terribly and I was scratching myself a great deal of the time. Every experience like this only reinforced past memories of the joy to soak oneself in a warm soapy bath or of having a hot shower. I admit to harbouring saturnine and doubting moments while in solitary confinement. My emotions occasionally overcame my resolution to remain positive; tears ran down my cheeks on days recalling important dates such as my birthday; or my mother and father, my younger brother, three sisters and I often wondered what they would be doing at this precise time back in England.

My food usually consisted of two small bowls of rice with tea each day. Not the most salubrious of diets and I knew that my health would deteriorate rapidly unless circumstances were to alter. I had no spoon or eating implements and the rice was served in a small metal tray. The starvation would, over the time I was incarcerated, hasten the demise of many a good man. The cell furniture, if one defines it as such, consisted of three wooden planks side by side, which were slightly raised above the concrete floor. This was my bed and it was secured at one end by a piece of wood that I assumed was the pillow. The toilet facility was an empty ammunition box placed in one corner and the stench from this permeated the entire cell, every hour of every day and night. All prisoners in solitary were forced to carry these boxes out every morning to empty them while under armed escort. I had no toilet paper or any other aids for daily grooming and basic hygiene that Westerners were accustomed to. Absolutely nothing except the few dirty items of clothing I wore. After emptying our toilet boxes we were immediately returned to solitary. On the return to my cell, there were times when I was able to snatch a few leaves from a tree to use as toilet paper. The cells were so small that there was virtually no prospect of exercising our bodies apart from some muscle tightening and stretching of my limbs that I remembered from the physical fitness exercises I had learned at Woking Grammar, and from information about general health when I had enlisted with the RAF. This was only possible if the guards were not watching and when left alone in the cell.

Every time any Japanese guard or officer, sometimes in soft soled rubber boots, walked past a cell door, a prisoner had to stand immediately and then bow in Japanese form to them or he would be severely punished. This still applied if a guard walked by during the night, which meant on these occasions our sleep was disturbed.

One particular day, I had bowed twenty-two times by early evening because a guard had repeatedly walked up and down the cellblock. On the last occasion, I stood up ready to bow as this guard walked by again, but he did not stop to observe me and kept walking; on the way to his barracks I assumed, so I sat down again on my wooden bed. The guard had not left the Block, but had crept quietly back to my cell and noticed I was sitting down. He unlocked the door and entered the cell. He yelled '*kiotsuke*' (attention); which I obeyed. He immediately began thrashing me over my body with a knotted leather strap in one hand, which stung terribly with each stroke. With his other hand free, he hit me a number of times over my face with his closed fist. I could not retaliate or flinch a muscle because my punishment would have been more severe and my term of solitary confinement, if I survived the beating, lengthened.

This was by no means the only beating I received during my time in solitary. On average I was set upon at least twice a week by a guard; this was just the norm for the Nips treatment of us. Sometimes I thought this might have been partly due to the look of loathing I think my countenance periodically revealed, despite the effort to mask my genuine feelings towards these nefarious people. Despite my physical condition, which was daily weakened by confinement, a mix of fear, rage and frustration simmered within me. I often thought, during and after these beatings, that I strongly desired, and could so easily, have lifted any of these 'little yellow b******s' and with immense gratification thrown them across the cell room.

There are three further experiences of particular importance I must mention while I was kept in solitary.

First, throughout most of my incarceration in this cell there lived a spider with its web spun in one of the ceiling corners. It was fascinating to observe the occasional movements of this arachnid, seemingly wandering with purpose across its web as if it were on patrol. I imagined that this was not unlike a Japanese sentry during their surveillance of prisoners. Whenever this spider moved with remarkable alacrity to attack and kill any insect that found itself entangled in its web, I immediately thought of a Nip guard violently beating me. Occasionally an insect would escape from the web and I wondered if I would eventually be in a position to flee from the clutches of my enemy. From time to time, I mentally talked to this little creature and watched it for many hours thinking that if it could survive, then I hoped I could too, no matter what punishments were meted out to me by the Japanese, whom I was increasingly coming to see as being more degraded and merciless than any savage presently living on earth.

Second, not being privy to 'normal' human communication and contact, with only visits by our 'abnormal' natured Nippon guards, I expended numerous hours going over in my mind the many experiences I had been through since the outbreak of war. I thought of the emotional torment that my family must be experiencing, of my friends, my future outlook and how it all came to this. As part of these muses, on the vicissitudes of life, most of the PoWs in Rangoon Gaol retained some favourite songs, poetry, novels, films, quotes and lines from the Bible, or hymns that we would recall at various moments in our woebegone habitation. I, too, had some things that possessed a personal significance for me. These became important to me during my lowest ebb. A religious faith, or just the powerful words in many scriptures, was an important part of many a PoWs inner strength. These moments were, I believe, generally considered to have driven PoWs to pursue a positive belief in survival; to live another day, despite the seeming lack of divine intervention to destroy our enemy.

I had been raised in a Christian family (Church of England) and was infused with my Western heritage. One hymn in particular that I was very fond of then, and which I cherish to this day, was *Abide With Me*. I had learnt this hymn as a choir and altar boy at St Mary's

Church in my home village of Horsell in the early 1930s. The lyrics are as follows and what I could recall at different moments, and sang in my mind throughout my incarceration, I believe provided me with some solace.

> Abide with me; fast falls the eventide
> The darkness deepens; Lord with me abide
> When other helpers fail and comforts flee
> Help of the helpless, O abide with me.
>
> Swift to its close ebbs out life's little day
> Earth's joys grow dim; its glories pass away
> Change and decay in all around I see
> O Thou who changest not, abide with me.
>
> Not a brief glance I beg, a passing word
> But as thou dwell'st with thy disciples, Lord
> Familiar, condescending, patient, free
> Come not to sojourn, but abide with me.
>
> Come not in terrors, as the King of kings
> But kind and good, with healing in thy wings
> Tears for all woes, a heart for every plea–
> Come, friend of sinners, and thus abide with me.
>
> Thou on my head in early youth didst smile
> And, though rebellious and perverse meanwhile
> Thou hast not left me, oft as I left thee
> On to the close, O Lord, abide with me.
>
> I need thy presence every passing hour
> What but thy grace can foil the tempter's power?

Who, like thyself, my guide and stay can be?
Through cloud and sunshine, Lord, abide with me.

I fear no foe, with thee at hand to bless
Ills have no weight, and tears no bitterness
Where is death's sting? Where, grave, thy victory?
I triumph still, if thou abide with me.

Hold thou thy cross before my closing eyes
Shine through the gloom and point me to the skies
Heaven's morning breaks, and earth's vain shadows flee
In life, in death, O lord abide with me.

To pass the many long hours, I also recalled and visualised, with as much detail as I could muster, of walking into St Mary's Church during a Sunday service, or entering the front door of my family home, hearing voices and seeing familiar faces that I knew. How could I not remember, given my desire for even one fulfilling meal from the Japanese, the satisfaction of sitting down to indulge in freshly baked bread, spread with a thick layer of butter; scones with jam; hot cups of strong tea with milk and sugar; indulging in a traditional Sunday roast dinner, or strolling along the streets and lanes of the peaceful village of Horsell, amidst the verdure of Surrey all of which I dearly longed to see and feel again? At the time, these recollections seemed a relatively short duration from my past and right now I was in dire circumstances. I have no doubt, when recalling this part of my incarceration, that these reflections were beneficial to my 'state of mind.' Doctor Mackenzie, who will be mentioned further in my recollections, wrote that our Japanese captors set out to: 'produce in the prisoners a state of mental confusion and physical weakness that left them nothing but nervous wrecks. They deliberately set out to turn their prisoners into invalids, incapable of further military or civilian service'.[34]

Third, interrogation and torture of many PoWs, particularly officers and some NCOs, including myself, became a routine and expected part of the Nips' treatment of us. During my time in solitary, I occasionally heard cries of pain issuing from other PoWs in the block; caused, I suspect, from being interrogated and beaten, or perhaps the result of pain from earlier punishment. Some of these auditory memories have remained with me all my life. My interrogation took place on two separate occasions while in solitary. The first of these occurred within two days of arriving. I was given one meal of rice and water over the first twelve hours. On the second day, suffering from stomach cramps due to a lack food and feeling the effects of dehydration again, I was taken to the commandant, Coshima if I recall, and was questioned following a similar procedure as when I had first been captured. I gave only my name, rank and service number. By now, this treatment was revealing itself as a characteristically rebarbative trait among our enemy. After questioning, and hoping my dissimulation worked, I was returned to a single cell. I was exhausted, hungry and extremely thirsty.

A short time later, three Nip guards brought in a dish of partly cooked rice and more drinking water than I had been given with any other meal. They left me temporarily while I ravenously consumed this food and drank all the water. At this point, my stomach already felt slightly swollen. The partly cooked rice was obviously expanding. About thirty minutes later the guards returned and, while standing over me and restraining my arms, forced me to eat more rice. When I refused to eat, one of the guards punched my face and warned me to continue eating. Another guard then started to push additional handfuls of rice into my mouth. I was then forced to drink a further quantity of water; much more than I required. At the end of this treatment, and now uncomfortably bloated, I was held down on the cell floor while a guard jumped onto my stomach and pushed his heels in as hard as he could manage. In time, I learned that this form of water and rice torture was perpetrated on many PoWs in Japanese prison camps and was another favoured form of punishment. When the guards returned me to my designated cell I was severely nauseous and had to lie down for some time to recover.

My second experience of torture occurred several days before I was released from solitary. I was asked once again to write down the details of my mission as I had previously done when first captured; this was to be handed to the Commandant. I wrote down, as accurately as I could remember, the same information as before. Some time later, four guards entered the cell. I was taken to what were called the 'Punishment' cells, which I later found out were in Block 4. I had not been to this compound before and I had no idea of what to expect, but I suspected that further interrogation or punishment was in the wind. Once inside I was taken to an empty room and my fear gained momentum. I was tied down and asked further questions, which I refused to answer. I was held by three sentries while a fourth guard pushed a slither of extremely sharp bamboo under my two large toe nails and partially lifted the nails. I was told by an interpreter that I had not told the truth, which I denied. The interpreter looked at me for several seconds and then gave orders for me to be returned to my cell in solitary.

Again, this method of torture was also not uncommon to many Japanese PoWs and it was known that some victims had finger and toe nails removed entirely in prison camps. I simply state that the pain was harrowing, and I still do not know to this day how I remained conscious. With tears running from my eyes, the sentries hauled me to my feet and, without treatment by any medical personnel, I was returned again to my cell. The agony I was in, trying to walk with those wounds, did not move the guards to any emotional response. Back in the cell, I managed to tear some small strips off part of my shirt to bind around my two toes to stem the flow of blood. I left this on until I was released from solitary. Within twenty-four hours my damaged toes revealed signs of infection, with pus forming on the wounds and a throbbing discomfort as the hours passed. I had virtually no sleep throughout this period, except when sheer exhaustion overcame me. I have lived my life since the war viewing my deformed toe-nails, which always grow into an unnatural mass. To this day, whenever I put on a pair of socks or look at my toes, it is not hard to visualise the Nip guards mutilating them.

Captain Tazumi Motozo another commanding officer of Rangoon Gaol arrived in early 1944; in my opinion, his attitude towards PoWs was no different to his predecessors, except towards the very end of our incarceration. To this day, I sometimes wonder if Motozo knew that the tide of the war was veering advantageously towards the Allies by the time of his command at Rangoon, and so restricted the number and extent of atrocities being inflicted on us in one particular way. The quantity of rations given to prisoners on some days in the compounds was increased and occasionally included portions of fish and tobacco products. Despite this welcome, though relatively temporary joy, many episodes of beatings and torture were still carried out. The Chief Medical Officer of Rangoon Gaol, Lieutenant Onishi Akio, rarely paid any attention to the plight of captured servicemen. This was despite repeated and emphatic complaints throughout our incarceration by our own doctors and high-ranking Allied officers about the dire circumstances of inadequate medicines and equipment essential to treat the medical problems that afflicted the PoWs.

Beevor rationalises this mindset of cruelty as a part of the Japanese soldiers' upbringing in the militaristic society of the era. He argues that the Japanese dehumanising process stems, in part, from their training; not as a means to display support for their Emperor, but more as a reflection of honour towards their own family and local communities.[35] This explanation resonates to some extent with an article in the November 2002 issue of FULCRUM, the magazine devoted to the Japanese Labour Camp Survivors Association of Great Britain, which cites extracts from Japanese history pre-1922:

> *The chief unit of social life in Japan is the family, the formal decisions of whose 'council' are, in many instances, recognised by the State as practically the equivalent to a legal enactment. The actions of the individual are largely subordinated to considerations of the family approval and advantage, particularly in such matters as marriage, business career, etc.*
>
> *The safe return home of a soldier from a victorious campaign was often regarded as less desirable than death on the field of battle, for the latter brought undying glory to the family name, since the sacred memorial tablet placed in the family shrine provided a perpetual record of the sacrifice of one of its members to the countries cause, and not only gave satisfaction to the living, but also served as a source of eternal pleasure to the spirits of the departed ancestors.*
>
> *These ideals, however, are slowly disintegrating, under the influence of an individualism which is permeating nearly every class of society. Moreover, the growth of democracy is accompanied by an increasing disinclination for military service and by a steady revolt against the rule of a military autocracy which has for so long held sway over the nation's affairs.[36]*

Stibbe views the Japanese at this time as uncivilised and, despite having good characteristics as well as bad, they lacked a Christian ethos which he claims stems from their relatively short contact with the Western world. He believes the Japanese possessed something of a childish personality, with an inferiority complex, and inwardly, were not seen as being on equal terms with their Western counterparts and therefore inflicted gross cruelties on their enemies with a fanatical zeal. He also argues that the Japanese people as a society, over several generations, could evolve into a civilised nation if their fanaticism were removed.[37]

Hope for the best, prepare for the worst

After thirty days of solitary confinement I was released and able to reunite with mostly British and a few Australian and American forces men. All the main prison Blocks, as far as I knew, comprised a ground and first floor. The windows had metal bars fitted to them but no glass. From information most PoWs received during incarceration, the compounds had about five rooms on each level and accommodated approximately thirty men each, depending on the number of newly arriving prisoners and the number of men who were ill or recently died. We had access to a water trough at one end of this block with which to wash ourselves with cold water, usually by dousing ourselves. This did not happen every day.[38] I had no soap or shaving supplies, and one or two prisoners had managed to hold onto a well-used razor blade, or a sharpened piece of metal, which was occasionally shared to remove some of our facial hair. We had no toothbrushes, toothpaste or toilet paper; absolutely nothing other than the few pieces of clothing we had on and over time, most of this became vermin infested and full of patches. My boots had long since been taken from me by our captors.

When I was released from solitary I was in a poor physical state, having lost many pounds because of the Nips policy of slow starvation of its prisoners, and the inevitable consequences of malnutrition. The wounds on my two large toes needed urgent medical attention and I was fortunate in one sense, as we had at least two British and a Canadian doctor to care for Western PoWs. I first met Doctor MacKenzie in Compound 3; he took one look at my infected toes and damaged nails and told me the nails would have to be removed. I was examined thoroughly for any other cuts, sores and infections, internal and external damage, that I was, or could be, suffering from. There was a possibility of gangrenous infection in my toes and, because I had no painkillers, I had to bite down on a strip of wood while the nails were removed in one fast motion with a pair of tweezers. The agony during this procedure I will not attempt to describe. The doctor then cleaned and dressed the wounds as quickly as possible. I was placed in the improvised hospital section until my toes began to form a new growth without any further sign of infection. The nails never actually regenerated in a normal process of horizontal coverage but rather as a developing, upwards mass. When I eventually had proper footwear following liberation, my two large toe nails, and throughout my remaining life, have always required a little extra attention.

Another doctor who I met when suffering with other medical conditions, which I'll mention later, was Major Ramsay, who took control of the hospital in Block No. 6 following his release from solitary in late 1943. We all knew the camp doctors, Major McLeod, Colonel MacKenzie and Major Ramsay, saved a good many men from dying. Apparently two of the earlier incarcerated Indian doctors in the Indian Block found the conditions in the camp 'unacceptable,' and I suspect may have done a deal with the Japanese officers in Rangoon; they left the prison in April 1943. There were other Indian doctors who were incarcerated and, also confronted daily with death and disease, had to perform medical care with limited resources and managed to save many of their fellow countrymen. Doctor Ramsay was the primary surgeon for most serious cases related to Western PoWs and, as far as I was aware, became responsible for organising the smuggling of stones, which held traces of copper sulphate, into the prison by men on work parties. When extracted, the copper sulphate was crushed into a fine powder, dissolved, and then used to treat jungle sores of which I will mention later in my recollections.

Colonel MacKenzie, a British career army doctor in his early fifties, had been a prisoner of the Japanese since early 1942 and had suffered from a much longer period of solitary confinement than I. Rangoon was the second prison in which he was incarcerated. From my own observations and from information that did its rounds in the camp, he was not in a good state of health. All doctors provided PoWs with much essential information we needed to better survive in the camp, beyond advice on hygiene and health issues prevalent in the prison. Everyone I met spoke very highly of our senior officers, including Brigadier Hobson, who was another of the longest serving and surviving PoWs. My initial impression of Hobson, and of every other PoW as far as I knew, was that he displayed the archetypal disposition of the strong and indomitable British soldier; as intrepid as any, who spoke in a forthright but unwavering manner, giving the impression of one who could never be suppressed by his enemy. He became an inspiration to many throughout our incarceration. By early 1944 however, so many of the PoWs were very ill and worn down by their treatment.

Throughout our captivity in Rangoon, the Japanese authorities had all Red Cross parcels and medical supplies stopped, so even the most basic of personal items like razor blades or soap became for many of us a past memory in our minds. We received no papers or magazines to keep up with affairs either at home or around the world, so we had the fear of not knowing the possible fate of our own families. Far more distressing though was the suppression of all letters and parcels from our families, friends or official correspondence and likewise, we could not communicate to the outside world. Our world now revolved almost entirely within the walls of Rangoon Gaol. The only news, and this was always limited, that was considered reliable was usually when a PoW with recent information of current events was sent to Rangoon. The *Greater Asia* (propaganda) paper printed by the Japanese that found its way into our prison was immediately discredited and understood as nothing more than an exercise to further undermine our morale. The Nips occasionally fed us information stating that Britain and her allies were being decimated by the Axis powers; that cities were being destroyed, battles waged and that we were being annihilated on all warring fronts. The Japanese believed they would one day rule much of the new world order that they sought to establish. There was some justification for this thinking as the old empires of Britain, France and the Netherlands fell, with the Japanese forces rapid and unexpected invasions throughout Southeast Asia. Burma had fallen to Japan in early 1942 and, with India in their sights, some prisoners had doubts concerning our future. Despite all this, the Japanese veneration of their Emperor Hirohito as a Deity would become nothing less than some diabolical and distorted notion to me.

The Japanese never released the names of their PoWs to the Red Cross, so we were always listed as missing. Our minds and our bodies had to respond and adjust accordingly to these new realities. If we did not, then many more men would have died and no one on the outside would have been the wiser if the Allies had not won the war. The one short letter I was allowed to write to my family during my incarceration never reached its destination anyway. The only information my family received while I was incarcerated, which I was to find out after liberation, was a letter from the London War Office informing them of my disappearance in April 1943. For two years my mother, father and three siblings suffered the anguish of not knowing what my circumstances were, except the possibility of my being a PoW. A second letter was eventually sent advising my family that I had been found alive in May 1945. I often thought of my parents, and younger brother Bob, (whether he was alive as a member of the Royal Corps of Signals) and if he had been in any major battles; of my three sisters and what their lives were like and again, if any of them had died. As much as I tried not to imagine the worst, these thoughts persisted.

In addition to not allowing any Red Cross parcels to be delivered, the Nips also refused representatives of the International Red Cross entry into their prisons. As no writing paper was readily available, some PoWs secretly kept scraps of material like empty cigarette packets, I later found out, to inscribe bits of information recording their experiences. This was a risky undertaking because when any PoW was caught, the punishment from our Japanese captors was severe. It was not unusual for some prisoners to be kicked in the groin for so called misdemeanours.

There were many occasions when news filtered through to us that purportedly came from other compounds including the Chinese Block. Some of the Chinese prisoners understood the Japanese language. A General by the name of Chee, who was much respected, was the senior officer in their block but he died of wounds inflicted by another Chinese PoW. News circulated on the grapevine that Doctor MacKenzie had finally been allowed to tend to General Chee but by that stage, his wounds had been ignored to the extent that little could be done to save him. We had our own channels of communication from one compound to another but caution was of extreme necessity. Despite the fear of being caught by our ever suspicious and watchful Japanese sentries we passed information between ourselves remarkably efficiently I thought.

Just being outside of solitary confinement was a terrific emotional relief. At least the air was clean and I could indulge in getting some direct sunlight onto my body when allowed outside the block. While we could not congregate in large groups, the changes in my circumstances from solitary confinement were, even by the standards we had to lower ourselves to, a welcome improvement. Being able to talk to other English speaking serviceman again was reassuring, and the camaraderie among us was critical to many of the men clinging on to the belief that the Allies would eventually regain the upper hand in the war and we would be freed. While we were denied the most basic of necessities required for our physical or emotional wellbeing, at least the mental torment was partly relieved by this group contact after so long in solitary.

I was also able to see my good friend from 99 Squadron, Paul Griffiths. How Paul had suffered in solitary too, with dramatic weight loss and a sallow complexion. What a joy it was though to see my friend still alive! There is a part of the human psyche that, despite experiencing atrocious and bleak conditions, and possessing no certainty of ones immediate future, can still find enough inner-strength and comfort from even one friend to generate a renewed sense of determination to survive. Paul recalled that after bailing out, he and the rest of the crew of our Wellington had decided to enter the first village they came upon and take their chances of being able to return to India. However, the Burmese locals informed the Nips stationed nearby. They were subsequently taken as PoWs and, like myself, transported to Rangoon Gaol. Paul told me what he knew of the Japanese and their pugnacious fanaticism for discipline as he viewed it. We discussed, one of numerous times amongst all prisoners, how to try and thwart some of the implacable punishment that the Japanese were intent on inflicting on us.

One of the rules insisted on by our captors was that all prisoners had to learn, as soon as possible, many Japanese words and expressions of command to address the Nips. I already knew several, and gradually learned much more as the months passed by. If our replies to the Japanese authorities were incorrect or unsatisfactory, whether we understood this or not, we were often beaten about the body with their hands or whatever implement a guard carried with him. They were also very fond of kicking us on our legs and shins. Each type of punishment invariably left cuts and bruises on our bodies. If we did not salute correctly, or answered a Nip sentry in a manner that displeased him, we were punished. We had to salute or bow, depending on their rank, to every sentry and officer in passing at all times, and usually refer to them as 'Master'. Roll call, *tenko*, was done every morning and early evening.

I witnessed many men being badly beaten for seemingly minor infringements like not bowing in the correct fashion, or not low enough, as I had previously found out. If we even attempted to defend ourselves then the punishment would be more severe. Some men were systematically punched on their faces, kicked repeatedly or other assaults including being hit with rifle butts, wooden clubs and even the buckles of belts. Newly arrived PoWs were warned by their fellow prisoners to never look a Nip guard in the eyes when being punished or the treatment would usually be longer and harder. I think nearly every prisoner became so used to witnessing or experiencing these episodes of daily violence and death among fellow PoWs, that some became conditioned to it. Inwardly, I knew most of us accumulated daily our rancour and contempt, while simultaneously managing to outwardly conceal this from our captors.

My bedding was some old rice sacks and bamboo matting spread on the floor. After several months, the clothing I had worn since first arriving at Rangoon had become threadbare and filthy with patches covering parts of my shorts. As these gradually began to disintegrate, I was issued with my new set of clothes. This consisted of a loincloth in the style of a bikini, my *fundoshi*, made of old cotton, blue coloured and with my PoW Number 59 stitched onto it. I also had a thin blue cap of the same material to wear. This was my only protection from the outside elements and without any footwear, like nearly every other prisoner, we were to sustain numerous complications from heavy labouring while consuming starvation rations.

As one of the higher-ranking NCOs, at times I was forced to take beatings from Japanese guards for some relatively minor infringements committed by other PoWs. One of the most violent guards, although violence here was a daily and expected occurrence in Rangoon Gaol, was a Private Koigetsu. During his time in Rangoon he was relentless in punishing as many of the PoWs he encountered as possible. The Nips were intent, and displayed, in our minds, a sadistic delight in meting out punishments, whether an offence, according to their terms, was justified or not. They did not need any justification because we prisoners were designated as having forfeited our rights to be treated as servicemen under the Geneva Convention. According to the Japanese 'Code of Military Conduct', their interpretation of this convention was irrelevant to the survival of their enemies.

Official Japanese policy encouraged brutality towards Prisoners of War by applying, post-war, the Geneva Convention with the proviso containing a limiting expression 'mutatis mutandis.' This was translated by the Japanese as 'with any necessary amendments', described by others as 'a bill to legalise tyranny.'[39]

The Japanese notion of what an 'honourable' soldier encapsulated differed from those of the Allied serviceman and women. Decency never entered into the equation. The Nips broke the spirits of some fellow Allied prisoners who appeared to just give up. If they did, we could never condemn these men and their tormented souls. For these colleagues of ours, their pain and suffering went on too long and in one sense, at least for some, I imagine that their passing came as a relief to them. Those of us who survived either somehow managed to retain our inner resolution, or were just simply fortunate that our bodies held out as we became ever more physically and emotionally debilitated and therefore susceptible to all manner of diseases and nervous disorders. One of the realities we faced was trying to create a new life inside our 'changed world' in the gaol. We only had what we stood up in and the support of our fellow inmates. We had to somehow overcome the horrors confronting us every minute of every day and to give up often meant to die. We prisoners were expendable. This was the simple fact.

The food outside of solitary confinement was only marginally better. The principle meal still consisted of rice, usually three times a day. The quality given to our cookhouse staff was for a long time a grain considered unfit for consumption by the Japanese.[40] While the quality varied from time-to-time, and sometimes included bran that was mixed like porridge, it was generally of a similar standard fed to pigs by the Japanese. There were days when some of our meals were prepared from vegetables, or they were included with our usual fare of rice. When vegetables were used as a soup, it was necessarily watered down to feed to the PoWs; the result being a very thin concoction with virtually no nutritional value for our bodies. For approximately every 200 men, only a few pumpkins and some marrows, or small portions of other vegetables including onions, beans and potatoes, were provided by the Nips. In a relatively short time, this diet resulted in massive vitamin and mineral deficiencies for every PoW. There was virtually no meat in our diet. Subsequently, many men died unnecessarily – particularly from beriberi. Doctor MacKenzie later wrote of this situation:

> *The Japs stubbornly refused to make the necessary changes in our diet to fight beri-beri. The principal constituent of our diet was polished rice and this was only supplemented by a few vegetables and a little tough meat.*'[41]

In an attempt to minimise this deficiency in our diets, two ideas were instigated. One was to grow some vegetables from small vegetable patches in some of the compounds. Doctor Mackenzie, with his resolute Scottish determination to try and improve the nutrition in the diets of as many PoWs as he could in Compound 3, had set about building a small vegetable patch to grow a few cabbages, spinach and a couple of other vegetables, but the Nips put an end to this after about a year. A germination station was established by a Corporal Tweedie, who successfully grew some beans to boost the amount of Vitamin B in the PoWs diet, but quantities were always insufficient. The Japanese guards controlled much of this operation, again to the ultimate detriment of the health of prisoners.

Secondly, men on work parties, both of their own volition or encouraged by others, tried to smuggle some food into the camp. Of this latter option, all PoWs on working parties outside the prison took great risks to do this. Despite best efforts, some prisoners eventually developed vision and hearing impairment from inadequate nutrition. The chronic and severely debilitating health problems included beriberi, dysentery, malaria, ulcers and jungle sores. These medical issues were exacerbated by the ever-present scourge of ring and thread-worms, lice and scabies. As medical equipment was virtually non-existent, there were at least two cases of amputations of limbs that had to be performed without anaesthetic. I believe some small quantities of morphine were obtained, but totally insufficient for these operations.

Notwithstanding these circumstances, I have found it difficult to explain to many people the effect of these privations on the human body and psyche. People who have never spent a single day of being forced to forgo a reasonable meal to fill their stomachs on demand; never experienced the unrelenting hunger-pangs that all prisoners of the Japanese went through continually; twenty-four hours a day, seven days a week, month after month, until this turned to a year and more, having to watch once fit and healthy men gradually reduced to haggard embodiments of skin and bones. Many men died soon after they became ill because of this diet. On the few occasions I have brought myself to speak of these experiences, I feel that some of my listeners took the view that I exaggerated the circumstances

we PoWs were confronted with every day we were incarcerated.
Even at night-time when I lay on my bedding, usually after an
exhausting day of manual labour, I regularly tried to force my mind,
and convince myself that my stomach was full, after consuming a
scanty and tasteless meal. If we arrived back from our 'coolie' work
after sunset, we were sometimes forced to eat our final meal of the
day in the dark. The Nips insisted that a 'blackout' of buildings be
enforced to minimise the risk of Allied air raids with the result that
many meals were often organised in a chaotic state.[42]

The desire for food was almost always in our thoughts, in addition
to the onslaught of a multitude of other problems that beset us day
after day after day. I would have to wait for two years before being
able to eat any substantial quantity of meat. This occurred only
three weeks before liberation by Allied forces and when the Japanese
comprehended that the end of their rule in Burma was nigh. While
in prison, we were provided predominantly with tea to drink. Some
prisoners, including myself, drank from improvised cups principally
of a cut section of bamboo, with its joint at the bottom intact to
hold liquids. There was never any milk, and sugar was given in such
minute quantities that, like almost everything that Westerners were
accustomed to, we simply went without.

There was no privacy among prisoners and inevitably there were
squabbles as some PoWs reached their breaking point. From these
outbursts it did not take us long to realise that there was nothing
to be done other than accept our circumstances and, at least in the
short term, it was beneficial to focus on, and channel our energy into,
outwitting the Nips wherever possible. Even in our squalid rooms
the Japanese sentries would regularly search every square foot for
any items that may have been stolen from their supplies, obtained
through internal or external bribes, or brought from outside the
prison by work parties. If any items were found, they would be taken
from us. If any sentry discovered stolen items, retribution was swift.

Stibbe recalled one incident when some bars of soap were discovered missing from the supply store in the prison. There were beatings and a number of PoWs were forced to stand to attention in the hot sun for at least three hours on two separate occasions.[43]

Slave labouring

Our captors forced as many prisoners as possible to undertake 'work duties' no matter what the conditions were like in this tropical environment. Most days were either very hot and humid, or consisted of heavy downpours of rain lasting days, or even weeks, at a time during the monsoon season. Only those who have witnessed these events can understand such deluges of rain and violent electrical storms. Without fail, the monsoon season strikes in all its fury from the southwest in May, covers Burma and continues into October. Never have I witnessed such downpours that turn unsealed areas of ground into layers of mud and flooding within a matter of hours. The humidity levels exacerbated our misery and the spread of skin diseases was ever apparent at this time.

We usually worked six or seven days a week and had one day off a month. The working day commenced at 6.00 am and our only means of getting a wash was at the block's communal water supply. There were many times when the main water supply to the prison broke down and at these times we usually had to go without even a basic wash. Soap was never provided and, for Westerners used to relatively good hygiene standards, this situation became another luxury we had to forgo. We had to be satisfied with dousing ourselves with some cold water to remove the worst of the grime off our bodies. We simply had to modify our habits and adapt to changed circumstances by improvising where and when possible. Some PoWs occasionally managed to circumvent the paucity of basic items with the odd bar of soap, which they concealed in their clothes if they were detailed to work on the nearby docks unloading ships. Over time, a number of books were obtained by these same methods until the Japanese guards eventually realised, from their meticulous, regular audits and searches, not to mention their ever present distrust of us, some items were not accounted for. To overcome this, they started to search all PoWs after the work parties returned to prison.[44]

Work parties were nothing more than units of slave labour that were directed to aid the Japanese with their war effort. There were days when we were forced to go out before day break without any breakfast and forced to toil for up to twelve hours in these conditions with a single half hour break to consume a scanty lunch of rice. If we had breakfast, it usually consisted of boiled rice and tea. We had a parade line up in the morning at 7 am, and another in the evening for tenko (roll-calls). As part of this morning procedure, we had to line up outside our rooms, usually accommodating about thirty men, and those PoWs considered fit (if one could stand), would almost always be forced to join a working party. Every one of these working parties was excessive and always included some very sick men, but the Nips did not consider this to be of any consequence. Many times, when we were lined up and standing to attention as required, one or more of the sentries would step in front of every PoW and give them a hard slap on each side of the face.

All prisoners had to memorise many Japanese words and numbers. The first two words I had learnt were *butai temare* (halt) and *kiotsuke* (attention). If we did not reply in the correct Japanese terms, we were often beaten with their fists, open slaps on our faces or hit with a stick of bamboo, a wooden club or their rifle butt. If a prisoner flinched then it was not unusual for a guard to lash out again and punch or kick the poor soul repeatedly. I can recall seeing some PoWs hit by a split bamboo pole and as most of us had virtually no clothes on to speak of, the wounds caused by these floggings took a long time to heal if they became infected. Many of these wounds left scars on prisoners' bodies.

The men in working parties were given a 'pittance of a wage', equivalent to about two pence (at 1940s rate) a day, which was considered very reasonable by the Japanese authorities for their 'Coolie' labour. NCOs and officers received a fraction more. The Japanese still deducted a portion of the 'wages' paid to their prisoners, including all officers and NCOs on the basis that these deductions were redirected towards the Japanese war effort. With this little extra money, some of the food we managed to purchase included a few chicken and duck eggs, which provided a much needed addition to our diet; albeit a too rare occasion. There were times when cheroots (cigars) were bought from local Burmese and Indians. Because many of the prisoners, including myself, had smoked prior to imprisonment, we experimented by drying banana leaves and trying to make cigarettes from them. The taste was very unpleasant, so we took to mixing some of the cigar tobacco with crushed banana leaves to eke out our supply for as long as possible. Sometimes we used the dried banana leaves to roll our cigarette tobacco in. I even started to experiment with small amounts of crushed bark and leaves picked up on my way to and from our work sites. Many of the men made their own pipes, usually from a section of bamboo or a small section of wood.

Because of the distances involved, some of our work-parties were taken to and from prison in the back of trucks and, on our return, we usually had the same, monotonous fare of a small helping of rice. Meals were often cold and most days our cooks served up a thin soup of pumpkin and marrows. Rarely, there was a fragment or two of meat, often about the size of one's fingertip, of beef, pork or chicken included in our meal. After the evening roll call we had a few hours to mingle with each other before the bedtime curfew of 10.00 pm, which was strictly adhered to every night. We were not allowed to talk or make any disturbance under threat of further beatings or some other form of punishment. We sometimes did manage to speak to those nearest to us in a quiet whisper and conduct informal discussions, or important information and news could be circulated in this manner.

The work parties went on every month we were in prison and, as more prisoners fell ill and died around us, our lives just got harder. A number of these sick men were taken to Block No. 6 and we never witnessed their final moments of demise. Doctors Ramsay, MacKenzie and McLeod, the last two whom would suffer with failing eyesight during their incarceration, continually endeavoured to keep as many men off the daily work rosters demanded by the Japanese; primarily those prisoners who were severely ill or suffering from wounds. A lot of men, who by any standards should not have been part of a work party, were still impelled to endure up to twelve hours of back breaking labour. Sometimes members of a work party managed to procure a few medicinal items through bribes with one or more Nip guards. Several of the PoW officers tried to supplement the money available from their own resources to obtain extra food for all prisoners, but this was never adequate to stem the increasing incidence of diseases like beriberi. Most of the men who died in Rangoon Gaol could have been saved. For a doctor, witnessing the daily sights of once healthy young men dying, often by inches at a time and suffering with pain and discomfort became a devastating experience as there was little hope of the situation improving.

Escorted by armed Japanese sentries, we sometimes had to walk outside the prison to get to our work destination. Throughout the hot weather we were usually forced to walk on the roads that became so hot some days that it was a matter of necessity for many men to wear crude, self-made footwear, carved from bits of wood. There were bouts of sunburn on our upper bodies if we had no shirts to cover us. Many occasions, if a prisoner had not bowed to a sentry, or in an unacceptable manner, or there was some missing food unaccounted for, or some other infringement determined by our captors, another of the Nips punishment was to force us to stand in the hot sun for several hours. If a prisoner on work duty was ill the treatment still applied. This punishment of exposing us to the elements also occurred during some of the heavy torrential downpours in the wet season.

The first work party I found myself in had been instructed to build earth bunkers for Ack Ack Guns (Anti-aircraft guns) and an underground air raid shelter because Rangoon, though under Japanese control, was sometimes attacked by Allied aircraft during the dry season. One air-raid shelter was located in a local Rangoon school by the name of Nyomo.[45] When the air-raid shelter had been dug and supports put in, we had to shift the tons of soil and stones removed from the site to cover the shelter. Some of the earth we had to dig was placed inside old sacks or on improvised stretchers. If we were seen to be not working hard enough, a guard was always nearby to hit us with a rifle butt, a piece of bamboo, or a wooden club. The work was 'back breaking', filthy, arduous and exacerbated by the hot and humid weather. These were utterly exhausting days and those PoWs who could help support the more debilitated men never hesitated. When these bunkers were completed to the satisfaction of the officers, I was detailed to another working party and was required to dig a hole large enough to construct a building that would accommodate our captors' Headquarters.

Stricken with malaria

After six months of this work, towards the end of 1943, my body was badly malnourished; I contracted malaria and could not work. Symptoms can include fever, shivering, convulsions, joint pain, vomiting, anaemia and retinal damage. Most of the prisoners, including existing malaria patients, were not protected from mosquitoes due to the lack of the nets that could restrict the spread of this disease. At night-time we used whatever bits of clothing, sacking, socks and boots, if we had them, to keep the mosquitoes from biting us while we slept. Relatively speaking though, Malaria was, not a huge problem for the camp, and even the slightest reprieve from any potential health hazard was a blessing to prisoners.

Some Quinine found its way into the hands of working parties outside the prison. Doctor Ramsay kindly gave me Quinine which, given its very limited supply in the camp, meant some of the other PoWs might have to go without or received reduced quantities. Doctor Ramsay somehow managed to produce a form of 'home-made' quinine using a process of fermentation with poppy plants that found their way into the prison. I had severe pains in most of my joints but eventually broke the fever; I sweated profusely for several days as the disease subsided, and was finally given the all clear. Our doctors and their orderlies had to make judgement calls with every sick and diseased PoW, knowing that some would not survive. Death became a routine experience in Rangoon as dozens of once healthy Allied servicemen succumbed to the almost complete lack of nutritional food, hospital facilities and medicines that should have been provided, but were denied to our medical personnel.

Dysentery

As the monotony and adversity continued each day, I was sent back to labour in the regular working parties. At this point I had to struggle ever harder to get through. Already weakened by malaria, I went down with dysentery a few weeks later at the end of January 1944, and thought I would not recover; I was told later by several of my fellow inmates, who were already accustomed to death and disease in prison, that they were of the same opinion. On that occasion I think there were times when I felt so ill that all I wanted was for the pain and misery to end; whatever the outcome this process took. Within two weeks the little muscle and flesh I had on my body quickly wasted away and I could see the outline of bones, including my rib cage, thinly covered with my skin. My joint bones looked like grotesquely enlarged protrusions. Given the poor sanitation conditions in the camp, many men were to suffer from this condition and some died. The stomach and bowel pains were terrible and I frequently passed faeces that were nothing more than fluids. The loss of control over my bowel movements, sometimes well over ten times a day and during the night, meant the selfless volunteer hospital orderlies, prisoners also, showed enormous fortitude in caring for patients like myself. If I needed to use my bowels I was assisted, by one or more of our orderlies, to a makeshift latrine in the corner of the room, which was another empty ammunition box. Although this was usually emptied each day and rinsed with water, there was never any disinfectant given to our medical staff by the Japanese.

The way the volunteer prisoner orderlies withstood the pungent smells and continual cleaning of patients suffering from beriberi and dysentery was a credit to them. Survivors, including myself, will always remain deeply indebted to these hardy and dedicated men. The Jap sentries sometimes brought in torn pages from some books or magazines, always insufficient quantities, for our hospital orderlies to assist with the cleaning of body fluids for patients, but never any proper toilet paper, soap (except for a few small occasional bits) nor sufficient clean clothing, although some old sacks or blankets were used when they could be obtained. These were never enough for the treatment of dozens of ill prisoners. There was always a shortage of hot water to sterilise bits of cloth and one of the reasons for this is because the Japs only provided small amounts of wood to use only for cooking food. I was not alone in thinking that any atrocity generated in the minds of our adversary was permissible for them to try and break our will to live; to revel in some perverse program of reducing each prisoner to a broken specimen of their former self.

Conditions throughout the hottest months were difficult enough but when the wet monsoon weather, with ever-higher humidity levels, swept across Burma the situation in prison just got worse. The grounds outside our compounds turned to a muddied sludge. As so few prisoners owned proper footwear, we still had to walk in this filthy sediment to and from the latrines day and night. We had no clean water to wash our feet with, except to wipe the worst of the mud off before entering our living quarters, life became ever more miserable and morale shaking. The doctors were given virtually no medical supplies in the form of drugs, instruments or gauze for wounds, and very little hot water for sterilisation. Medical instruments were almost all handmade improvisations used by hospital staff. Despite constant requests and complaints by our own medical officers, Doctor Mackenzie stated that the Japanese Commandant Coshima ignored demands for assistance. Items were so scarce that one of the improvised scalpels was made from a used razor blade and used for smaller incisions on things like boils and abscesses.[46]

The death of Paul 'Griffo' Griffiths

In early 1944, I was also confronted with my close friend and confidante, Paul Griffiths, being struck down with beriberi and lose his struggle to survive. At the time, we were both in Block 6, the hospital quarters at this time for all white PoWs. Paul reminded me in many ways of my younger brother Bob; not in physical looks but he was of a similar demeanor. I had been so incredibly fortunate, or perhaps it was sheer willpower that had kept me going beyond what I had considered possible; sadly, when Paul developed beriberi, his body could not maintain the struggle any longer. Beriberi is caused by a deficiency of Vitamin B; a lack of thiamine affects many systems of the body including the heart, nerves, muscles and digestive tract. Some prisoners referred to beriberi as the 'Third of the Trio'. It was a couple of weeks into the New Year of Paul's confinement and I made my way to his makeshift bed when possible. I talked with him about his family back home in England, of future plans and imagining what we would do if and when we got out of Rangoon Gaol alive. These moments were usually of short duration and his speech sometimes less lucid. When Paul was coherent with his thoughts, he more than once asked me to visit his family in England should he not recover. Conversations of this nature elicited many emotions. Nearly all prisoners, including Paul and I, were in our early twenties and we wanted yet to live a long, happy and hopefully, purposeful life.

Fatigue and joint pain exacerbated Paul's discomfort, though he rarely complained. Paul's ailing health, and witnessing his demise first-hand, upset me terribly. His legs, hips, genitals and torso became increasingly swollen. Towards the end I could barely recognise Paul with his bloated body. Occasionally beriberi victims wasted away to skin and bones; not unlike our dysentery sufferers. Either way, many men in that prison died simply through a lack of adequate food and medical necessities denied us by our captors. On one occasion I pleaded with the doctor to provide some extra food for Paul, such as an egg. My request was denied however, given there were always patients of varying degrees of illness. Patients were prioritised on a case-by-case basis and some of the rations from relatively 'fit and healthy' men were already being redistributed to feed to those most ill. Bitterly, I understood this, for our doctors could not be held responsible, and simply had to accept the almost certain outcome for many ill prisoners.

Paul passed away on 14 February 1944, less than a year after his incarceration, and was buried in Rangoon War Cemetery. I was not allowed to attend the burial ceremony outside the prison walls, such as it was, when Paul was lowered into his grave. Even though I was very weak myself and not fully recovered from dysentery, I wanted to be present at Paul's burial. My last memory of this juncture was when prisoners lined up in the compound, as was done for all Allied servicemen on such occasions, and gave a final salute to Paul as his body was taken out of the prison.

Sometimes the bodies were covered in old blankets or, as with Paul, stitched up rice sacking and on rare occasions, a very rudimentary wooden casket was constructed. A well-used Union Jack was sometimes draped over the bodies of our dead comrades. The indignity and insults shown by the Nips towards our own dead servicemen was unforgivable. One of our Officers from the prison led this small burial party and I inwardly said my farewell and final tribute to Paul with lasting sadness. Paul will always be remembered by those who knew him as an intelligent, brave, loyal and decent man. To die so young, simply through a deliberate policy of starvation, malnutrition and chronic ill-treatment, grinds away at my emotions even today in a way I can never fully comprehend. Even with an indomitable spirit, there are occasions when the physical body can hold out no longer. Paul was one of my closest friends at this time and to this day, I often recollect some of the sorties we flew together in the same Wellington, our time in the Middle East and, of course, our bail out into Burma and subsequent incarceration. I promised myself, and it was Paul's wish, that I would personally visit his family, on the assumption that they, and I, survived the war.

My turn for beriberi

Approximately six months following the demise of Paul, and with many more men in the prison also dying or becoming ill, my luck did not hold out. It was my turn to go down with beriberi. I was

23 years old and, knowing the relatively high death rate from this disease among men in the prison, I thought the odds were against my surviving. One could not help feeling morbid at times, and this was one of them. As the disease progressed, my arms, legs, hips and genitals also became swollen and I thought I must have looked something like a cartoon version of 'Popeye'. One night while still feeling very nauseous and, I am sure, also subject to bouts of hallucinations, a build up of fluid began reaching my lungs. The medical staff had provided me with a bamboo back support, constructed to keep the upper half of my body raised. I had, by this stage of the disease, no strength to speak of. I sweated profusely and was in almost continuous pain with my atrophied leg muscles and painful joints. Again, the prison orderlies were continually checking on my condition. Without warning, I suddenly needed to urinate and then did so several times during the night. The doctor explained that he believed I was going to pull through. His prediction proved correct, but now I looked utterly emaciated with no strength to walk, or even stand, without assistance.

Over the next couple of weeks I was given my usual fare of what passed as a vegetable soup and some rice, when I could keep it down. When I could walk a little, our doctor kindly placed me into the cookhouse for light duties to further assist my recovery. During this time, my daily workload in the kitchen was minimised to aid recovery. The chores were still arduous, given my debilitated condition, but our captors insisted that every Prisoner of War, if they considered it so, and unless our medical staff persuaded them otherwise, was required to perform some work duties, or there would be further repercussions directed towards PoWs to make up the daily roster of work party men.

Jungle sores, bed bugs, scabies and cholera

I need to mention the jungle sores that virtually every prisoner, as far as I know, suffered from at one time or another in Rangoon. I still retain a number of scars from this episode of incarceration. Often a slight cut, which when exposed to the filthy and humid conditions we lived in, resulted in a sore rapidly developing or proliferating to other parts of our bodies. Some men died from the quick spread of these open, pus filled sores exacerbated by our chronically depressed immune system. The jungle sores were painful and, as most of us never had any covering for our feet or legs, they were a serious and ever present problem for our medical staff to treat. As I have partly alluded to, the only cauteriser, and in fact only medicine available, was a solution of copper sulphate, dissolved into concentrations from one tenth to full-strength solution. This improvised cure was our sole remedy. Most sores were treated with the full-strength solution, which was very strong and painful when applied, often causing my legs to sweat below my knees, but the treatment generally was successful. Many of the abscesses and jungle sores, including mine, were usually cut with an old razor blade or a piece of sharpened metal. Our doctors had to improvise where possible in making surgical instruments.

Another constant tribulation throughout the prison was scabies and bed bugs, which I had first suffered with when in solitary. Scabies is caused by small mites that burrow into the skin causing red, itching lumps or blisters to form. The itching was chronic and when afflicted with this condition, the point came when most prisoners relented and had to scratch the scab or earlier scars, this made them bleed and temporarily eased the torment. Bed bug populations were far more prolific and a greater problem than scabies. The foul smell of decomposing blood after a night of being bitten by these creatures was highly unpleasant for the senses to wake to. Added to this was the presence of vermin, such as rats and mice, which would occasionally skitter through our cells despite efforts to control them.

We also had a visit by Cholera in the camp. There were at around ten deaths from the only recorded outbreak in Rangoon Gaol, and the bodies of these victims had to be cremated within the prison walls. Even the Japanese authorities were outwardly frightened of this virulent disease and actually provided our medical personnel with inoculations for prisoners.[47] I believe lime powder was also given to our doctors to assist with stopping this outbreak. We who survived this disease considered ourselves very fortunate, given the propensity of any infection to rapidly spread among us, while we were in such an infirm condition. My antipathy towards this ignoble, primitive race, as I viewed the Japanese at the time, grew exponentially. You cannot imagine the utter venom seething through the minds of many PoWs of what we would like to do to the Japanese guards, officers, and their medical staff had we the opportunity to do so; let alone their Emperor. the only way we might one day wreak our revenge on them was to keep our minds focused on surviving. It wasn't that some prisoners didn't, on occasion, think about attempting to escape, but the chances of surviving were so incredibly to our disadvantage.

Lighter moments in prison

When it was possible, throughout our long days and nights in prison, we still tried to retain morale-lifting memories of special significance for Westerners and made plans to replicate specific occasions. Christmas, New Years Day and birthdays remained an essential part of the dozens of topics we discussed among ourselves during our incarceration. To this end, when our Japanese 'masters' allowed us to, we organised entertainment in the camp. These were of an irregular occurrence due to our work parties being out almost every day and other more critical problems of sick inmates. Men in Block 5 we were more restricted than some of the other Compounds' PoWs, but we did have some moments of simple pleasures.

Our informal and amateur sing-alongs, of varying lengths, usually included a couple of soloists who sang renditions of some favourite songs. These moments would channel our thinking to something other than the monotonous and heart-breaking daily rituals. There were always men among us who retained a good memory for jokes and stories told at various times, whether inside the prison or outside on work parties. A few PoWs with a creative flair were able to surprise us with their own little ditties or poetry and naturally some of these were directed at ridiculing the Japanese. Our entertainment, though limited and basic, was the best we could produce under constant surveillance. If any guard was in a good mood, though this was a relative notion, we usually seized the opportunity to indulge ourselves in some activities outside normal duties and demands. Some quiz games were also organised throughout our captivity. Several handmade packs of playing cards and chess sets were used by PoWs, and one of the most popular pastimes was quoits; again improvised.

Christmas and New Year in the two years I was a prisoner were times when well known traditional Christmas carols had a unique effect. As soon as these were started, almost every man present would join in. *Silent Night* was probably the best known and one of our favourites; the words and music to this hymn were always somewhat haunting to sing and I know moved more than one PoW to tears. We occasionally finished these moments with a rendition of *God Save the King* and the Americans finale came with their national anthem: *The Star Spangled Banner*. One American airman in Compound 5 had managed to obtain a bible, as had Brigadier Hobson in Compound 3, which was used when and where possible, given the Nips restrictions on what we could or could not do. There were always several PoWs who knew a number of verses from the good book, including myself, and who could recite particular lines to try to alleviate our miserable existence, even if only in spirit. It was moments like these that proved beneficial to our camaraderie and imparted a temporary hiatus from the otherwise clockwork regularity of our despondent day-to-day existence.

Changes 'in the air'

In time however, and I always thought of myself as a relatively patient man, we knew that American, Commonwealth and British forces had not forsaken the Far East and were far from beaten, as our Nippon captors would have us believe. There were sightings at different times of Allied aircraft flying overhead. In 1943 a single aircraft lobbed a couple of bombs outside the prison but this was an isolated case at the time and it was not until early 1944 when increasing numbers of Allied planes, including American bombers, began appearing over Rangoon. The sight of these provided a welcome and much-needed lift to our morale, but the Nip authorities took the opposite view and anti-aircraft defences were strengthened in the city. As Allied bombings kept coming, the prison received an occasional hit – this was not the way we PoWs wanted to die after the hardships we were being subjected to. At least ten British prisoners were killed during one raid and around thirty of our fellow PoWs would eventually die from raids during our imprisonment.[48] Many more were also injured before we were liberated. At the very least, we realised the Allies were intent on driving the Japanese out of their conquered territories. It wasn't all going the right way for the Allies yet because there were still sightings overhead of Japanese fighter planes on some days.

Towards the end of 1944 some of the work parties received information, possibly from the local Burmese or Indians, that

Germany was on the retreat. Evidence that our fortunes might be improving for the better occurred during Christmas day of 1944 when a couple of Nip guards brought in some cigars to give to PoW Air crews in Block 5, a gesture previously unknown to us. Several of these men became ill because they had not had any tobacco to smoke for a long time. Any differences of attitude and questionable displays of compassion by the Nips towards us, given their absolute indifference to our plight to date, immediately set most of our minds racing. Something, either good or bad, was in the melting pot.

Early in 1945 there were reports from some fellow Indian prisoners that the Allies were moving towards Rangoon, with sightings of tanks. We were hopeful but with reservations. At least there were increased bombings by the Allies, so we were keeping all options open at this point that we might eventually be free of this 'Hell.' On 9 of April 1945, I celebrated my twenty-fourth birthday and the beginning of my third year in captivity. Even a handshake and a simple expression of best wishes to me from prisoners was a most wonderful gift.

Throughout April 1945, other developments indicated changes of some magnitude were afoot. A few pigs and bullocks were brought into the prison for slaughter, which became the first large quantity of meat in our diets since capture. We could not understand the reasoning of the Nips increasing our daily food supply. Some prisoners jokingly said we were being fattened up for some as-yet-unknown surprise. How does one react to this? The meat was cooked in high anticipations of indulging in the meal with great relish. Many of the prisoners, including myself, found the meat was far too rich to digest and this caused varying stomach problems for our now sensitive digestive tracts and stomachs for several days. Added to this, men in work parties, which I still went out on most days, were being given bits of food by some of the local Burmese population as we walked along the roads to and from our designated job. Even these small gestures did not seem to upset the Nip guards unduly. Given that inflation was now rampant in Rangoon, and I presumed in most of Burma, I wondered if these locals were always sympathetic to the Allies. Their seemingly great acts of generosity, given our abject state of existence, were possibly being enacted principally to stop any severe retribution being waged on them by our now advancing and militarily superior forces. During the last half of April, rumour spread that the Allies were only about forty miles from Rangoon. At this time there were increasing reports of pistols and cannon fire in the city. I thought that possibly even the civilian inhabitants of Rangoon had suffered enough of Japanese rule. Occasionally the compound buildings would shake from a close explosion.

At this time, particularly throughout March and April of 1945, the Japanese army was increasingly being denied supplies as the Allied forces struck back. Winston Churchill had instigated changes to Command operations in the Far East in October 1943. Lord Louis Mountbatten was placed in charge of South East Asia Command. Major General Slim was given command of the newly formed British 14th Army (sometimes referred to as the 'Forgotten Army'). The British 14th Army, the largest Allied Army of the Second World War, was in fact a multinational fighting unit that included three battalions of Ghurkas and large numbers of Indian soldiers. The reputation of the Ghurkas' fighting capabilities and loyalty preceded them, and it was said that the 'fearless' Japanese were themselves nervous of these Nepalese soldiers. Slim was popular with his men. Being an experienced soldier himself, he was aware of conditions those under his command could expect. Many soldiers often referred to him as 'Uncle Bill.' Specifically trained units for jungle warfare were also used as 'Long Range Penetration' forces into Burma and were named the Chindits. The 14th Army was well equipped with fit personnel and made rapid advances, moving south through Burma and defeating any Japanese forces they encountered.[49]

Two important battles that saw the beginning of the end of Japanese control in Rangoon were at Meiktila in early March and then Toungoo in central Burma. Many Japanese began to flee Rangoon and Burma as the 14th Army advanced southwards at this juncture.[50] Allied aircraft, both bombers and fighters, were also creating havoc for the Japanese and their allies. The Japanese had been ordered to fight to the last man against their enemy even when we knew, and our enemy also realised, the Allies were closing in on them. With reference to this code of honour and loyalty, individuals of the present and future must make up their own minds. It is sometimes mentioned that time erases memories and the past may be best left in the past. It is interesting that two authors writing nearly a quarter of a century apart provide somewhat different sentiments about the Japanese fighting spirit.

In 1989, Hudson stated that: 'the Japanese are a proud race, steeped in nationality, and have been told they are invincible from their cradles on. They are taught to die first before surrender.'[51]

Slattery, writing twenty-four years earlier in 1965 states:

> ... the Japanese had never been noted for the "honour" to which they gave so much lip service. Having broken the rules of warfare from the start, by attacking Pearl Harbour without a declaration of war and while Japanese envoys were actually "negotiating" with Washington, they weren't likely to shrink from slaughtering enemy soldiers who had humiliated them.[52]

Many Japanese had fled from Burma by the time the Allies finally retook control. The Japanese Commander Kimura, and many of his senior military aids, had instigated a retreat from Burma with soldiers and equipment. It was said that they fled against the Emperor's orders and disregarded their purported military code of conduct. During these developments around March and April

An Indian Snake (Cobra) Charmer, 1942.

'Newsreel' Pete, 1942.

Bill in Calcutta, 1942.

Double-decker bus, Calcutta style, 1942.

The train at Solan (a hill station near Simla) travelling through the surrounding hills in North East India, 1942.

RAF Billets at Solan, 1942.

Digri: Time out for some service personnel, a few days prior to commencement of bombing missions against the Japanese over Burma in November 1942.

Local Indian Service Personnel.

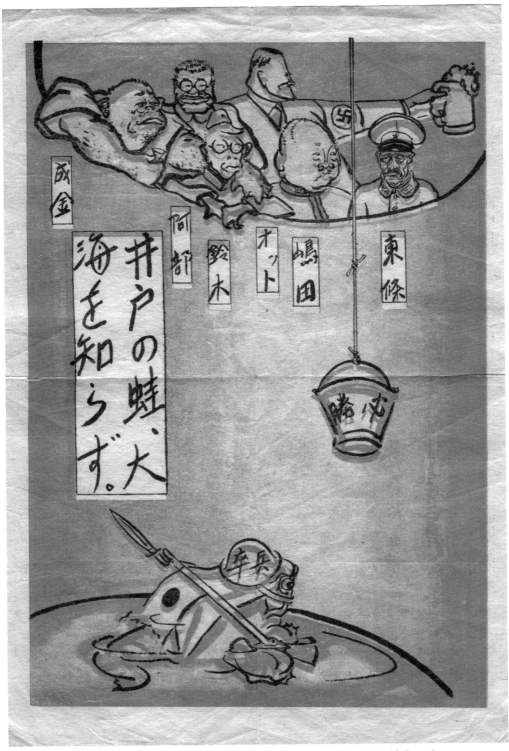

Copy of a propaganda leaflet (Nickel Raid) that was dropped into Burma by 99 Squadron.

ADVICE TO THE RELATIVE
OF A MAN WHO IS MISSING

In view of the official notification that your relative is missing, you will naturally wish to hear what is being done to trace him.

The Service Departments make every endeavour to discover the fate of missing men, and draw upon all likely sources of information about them.

A man who is missing after an engagement may possibly be a prisoner of war. Continuous efforts are made to speed up the machinery whereby the names and camp addresses of prisoners of war can reach this country. The official means is by lists of names prepared by the enemy Government. These lists take some time to compile, especially if there is a long journey from the place of capture to a prisoners of war camp. Consequently " capture cards " filled in by the prisoners themselves soon after capture and sent home to their relatives are often the first news received in this country that a man is a prisoner of war. That is why you are asked in the accompanying letter to forward at once any card or letter you may receive, if it is the first news you have had.

Copy of a section of the letter forwarded to immediate family concerning missing service personnel.

OPERATIONS RECORD BOOK

See instructions for use of this form in K. R. and
A. C. I. and notes in R. A. F. Field Service
Pocket Book.

of (Unit or Formation) .... *G. S. Graham* ....

Air Force (Ind

No. of pages used for day ....
Marriott .

Place.	Date.	Time.	Summary of Events.
DIGRI	1.4.43	09:00	Seven crews, Captained by F/L BROWN, F/L MACDONALD, F/O HOOD, F/O BENT, W/O SMITH, F/SGT. MUDRY, SGT SEYMOUR were detailed to attack HEHO aerodrome. Bad weather and snow rendered identification of the target formost crews. On return a signal was received at about 2300 hours from F/L MACDONALD that he was in trouble and that the crew were baling out of aircraft. the position then given was in the CHIN HILLS in enemy occupied territory. The crew members of F/L MACDONALD's crew was listed, and they were officially posted as missing: F/L MACDONALD (Pilot) SGT. GRIFFITHS (Nav.) F/O TOWNSEND (Nav.? obs) F/SGT. TATE (W/OP/AG) SGT. CARTER (W/OP/AG) and SGT. EDGLEY, (A/G).

Flight details for the Wellington Bomber and crew that Bill was part of after bailing out into the Chin Hills region of Burma on 1 April, 1943.

Rangoon Gaol in 1945, following the Japanese retreat from Rangoon.

収 容 所 Camp	馬寮 昭和 19年 3 月15日	番　號 No.	馬 VI 59	
姓　名 Name	William Albert TATE. ウイリヤム・アルバート テート	生 年 月 日 Date of Birth	1921.4.9.	
國　籍 Nationality	英	所 屬 部 隊 Unit	No. 625747. 99 Squadron. Royal Air Force.	
階 級 身 分 Rank	Flight Sergeant. 航空曹長			
捕 獲 場 所 Place of Capture	緬甸エナンダヤン南方三十哩	捕 獲 年 月 日 Date of Capture	昭和18 年 4 月 5 日	
父 ノ 名 Father's Name	William TATE.	母 ノ 名 Mother's Name	Elizabeth TATE.	
本 籍 地 Place of Origin	Birtley, NEWCASTLE-ON-TYNE, England.	職　業 Occupation	軍人	
通 報 先 Destination of Report	10, Kirby Road, WOKING, Surrey, England.	特 記 事 項 Remarks		

補 修 欄　Other Informations
本鋭ハ累記載ハ〔...〕ハ昭和20年4月29日ヲ西南方十粁（ビルマ）ニ於テ 解放ト推定セラル　　　　（VG 44）

Japanese Prisoner of War records for Bill, retrieved after the Allies retook Burma.

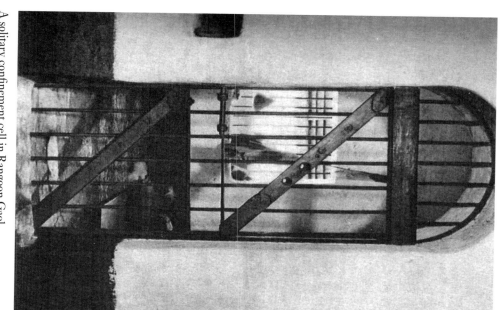

A solitary confinement cell in Rangoon Gaol.

Flight Sergeant Bill in India, January 1943.

Paul Griffiths, a close friend of Bill's from 99 Squadron who died in Rangoon Prison Camp from Beriberi. He is buried in Rangoon War Cemetery.

Major McLeod, the Canadian Surgeon with Corporal J Usher, whose right leg was successfully amputated without anaesthetic. Note the 'bikini' *fundoshi*.

Prisoners from Rangoon Gaol eat their first liberation meal.

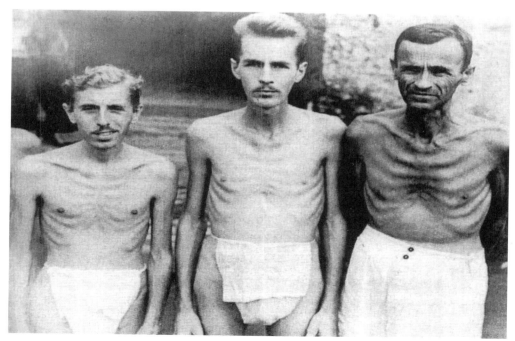

American POWs who survived Japanese incarceration in the Philippines.

Allied soldiers with grateful and elated former POWs who had been forced on the march out of Rangoon Gaol. Amongst this crowd is Bill himself. The photograph was taken near Pegu (now Bago), Myanmar.

PRISONERS OF WAR POST.
SERVICE DES PRISONNIERS DE GUERRE.
WOKING
8.45PM
8 DEC
625747. F/SGT. TATE. W,
R.A.F.
BURMA,
BRITISH PRISONER OF WAR,
C/O JAPANESE RED CROSS,
TOKYO,
JAPAN.

POST EARLY
FOR
CHRISTMAS.

MY DEAR SON,
AGAIN HOPING YOU ARE WELL. WE ARE ALL
LOOKING FORWARD TO YOUR RETURN SOON. HOME
MUCH THE SAME. ALL SEND LOVE.
MOTHER.

A telegram received by Bill from his mother after she had received the news that he was still alive.

Hope, still hope though the clouds hang low,
And keep your eyes uplifted.
For the sweet blue sky will soon peep
                                    through.
And the mists of doubt be lifted;
There never was a night without a day,
Nor evening without morning,
The darkest hour, is always the one
Which comes Before the dawning!

A short poem written by William.

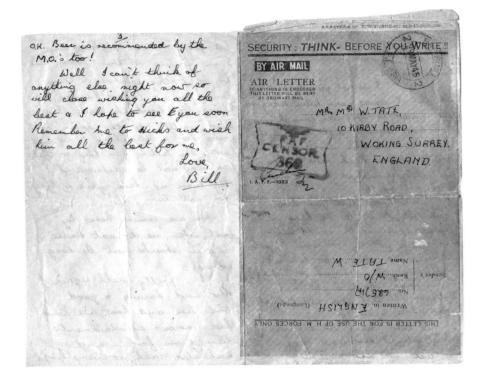

OK. Beer is recommended by the
M.O.'s too!
  Well I can't think of
anything else right now so
will close wishing you all the
best & I hope to see you soon
Remember me to Hicks and wish
him all the best for me,
          Love,
            Bill.

SECURITY: THINK- BEFORE YOU WRITE!!

BY AIR MAIL
AIR LETTER
IF ANYTHING IS ENCLOSED
THIS LETTER WILL BE SENT
BY ORDINARY MAIL

R.A.F.
CENSOR
368

I. A. F. F.—1083

MR. MR⁵ W. TATE,
10 KIRBY ROAD,
WOKING SURREY.
ENGLAND.

Sender's Name TATE W
Rank W/O
No. 625747

Written in ENGLISH (Language)

THIS LETTER IS FOR THE USE OF H. M. FORCES ONLY

26-5-45.

625747 W/O TATE W,
N°2 S.S.Q. R.A.F.
WORLI,
BOMBAY.

Dear Mother & Father
            I was not going to write at
all but I received your letter today &
have decided to reply even though you
should'nt have time to answer this.
I sent a cable this morning asking
you to cable back news of you all
but this letter and I have received
takes care of that.
      Well, I can't tell you how
wonderful it is to be back in a
civilised part of the world after
two years in the 17th century with
the nips. It all seems like a
nightmare now although it will
never fade like a nightmare.
However I'll tell you about that
when I see you.
      I have been to the committee
of adjustment here and have obtained
a list of all my personal

belongings sent to England and
I am writing to them from here
to see if they can send them
home for me before I arrive. My
flying log book the same. I've
also written to the Irvin 'chute
works for a caterpillar to be sent
home. I'm telling you this so that
you may not be surprised if
they turn up here again if they
do not turn up!
      We are coming home by
boat, when, we do not know,
but it should not be long,
we hope!
      I'm pretty well again
now and having a good
time here - and how. We have
had various entertainments
turned on for us and
unlimited cash, so everything's

A copy of the letter that Bill wrote to his family nearly four weeks after liberation.

Standing Committee of Adjustment,
R.A.F., Base Accounts Office,
R.A.F., South East Asia Air Forces.

5th June, 1945.

Ref:- BAO/1008/563/COA.

Dear Mr. Tate,

Your letter dated 24th May, 1945, was duly received which we acknowledge herewith.

Your son F/Sgt. Tate has visited this Committee and I am very pleased to tell you he looked remarkably fit and well. At the moment I can give you no guidance of his address but as you have already stated you have heard by wire and cable from him, it is quite probable that within the next few days you will be receiving some ordinary mail communication.

The hardships these boys must have endured at the hands of the enemy most certainly will have left some mark upon their character, but it speaks volumes for their powers of endurance and courage whilst in captivity, that they are able now to walk around free men, looking as fit and well as they do.

I know that this will be very cheering news to you and may I say that, I hope the reunion between you and your son will be a joyous and momentous one, and that it may take place in the very near future.

/JSD/VR.

Yours sincerely,

[signature]

Squadron Leader,
President.

Mr. W. Tate,
10, Kirby Road,
Horsell,
Woking,
Surrey,
ENGLAND.

A copy of the letter from the Standing Committee of Adjustment, RAF, South East Asia Forces.

MARRIAGE OF WARRANT OFFICER W. A. TATE

The marriage took place at St. Mary's Church, Horsell, on Wednesday last week, of Warrant Officer William Albert Tate, eldest son of Mrs. and the late Mr. W. Tate, of 10, Kirby Road, Horsell, and Miss Irene Eva Cox, only daughter of Mr. and Mrs. A. E. Cox, of 15, West Street, Woking. The Vicar (the Rev. F. A. Woodard) officiated, and Mr. P. England, at the organ, played 'The Wedding March.'

The bride, who attended Goldsworth School, has been employed as a clerk at the Woking Co-operative Society. The bridegroom, who has been in the R.A.F. since 1938, and is now on demobilisation leave, was also educated at Goldsworth School and at the Woking County Grammar School for Boys.

Given in marriage by her father, the bride wore a full length white satin dress with net veil, and a headdress of orange blossom. She also wore a necklace and carried red carnations and fern. The matron of honour, Mrs. Ivy Black, and the bridesmaids, the Misses Irene and Esther Tate (sisters of the bridegroom) and Miss Mildred Haycroft (friend), wore dresses of turquoise blue and gold, with headdresses of feathered tiaras. They carried bronze chrysanthemums and wore brooches, the gift of the bridegroom. The best man was Cpl. Robert Tate, R.C.S. (brother of the bridegroom), and the groomsman was Sergt. A. Black, M.M., Scots Guards.

A reception was held afterwards in the Horsell Parish Hall, about 60 guests attending. The honeymoon was spent at Ventnor, the bride travelling in a blue costume with wine coat and accessories.

Bill and Rene's wedding notice, 13 November 1946, as featured in *The Woking News and Mail*.

1945, the once strong ally of Japan and Indian National Army, the Burmese Independence Army, switched sides, obviously to save their own lives and also taking an opportunity to control Burma after the war.

In Rangoon Gaol Brigadier Hobson received news of Allied fighter planes carrying out sweeps along major routes including Pegu Road. This news spread like wildfire to every block. The frequency of air raids steadily increased both day and night. In the daylight hours we sometimes witnessed the aftermath of bombings when mushroom clouds appeared in the sky. Some of these were very close and near to, or on, the dockland area of Rangoon, which was probably less than five minutes walking distance from Rangoon Gaol. Most explosions were more distant including to the north of us. The sounds of bomb clusters rumbling in the distance made me happy and more positive, but I did not want to end my life as a casualty of an Allied aircraft dropping its bombs on us.

Throughout March and early April, as news in the prison continued to circulate that the Allies had retaken Mandalay and Meiktila, I often recalled the bombing missions that 99 Squadron had carried out on these targets in early 1943. As General Slim's 14th army was making its way through Burma, these frontline troops were on half rations and relied on transport of supplies being trucked in from the rear. This was a difficult operation coming just before the start of the monsoon season and, though we PoWs did not know it at this time, Slim's tank and air transport movements were already being impacted. The monsoon season in 1945 had started approximately two weeks earlier than expected. To a large degree, the British troops were dependent on food and ammunition being flown in by American transport aircraft, but much of this was about to be taken away for the United States operations in China. It was also known that Washington was not keen to be seen helping the British re-establish themselves in South East Asia.

In Rangoon the heat became more intense, both day and night, as the annual monsoon weather crept ever closer. Our nights were uncomfortably humid and it was difficult to get any sound sleep, even if only for a few hours. The ever-persistent mosquitoes kept up a constant humming noises, like a group of fighter aircraft circling round our bodies. Every now and then a curse would erupt from a PoW directed towards the mosquitoes and often the Nips at the same time. We could only talk in very low voices because the Nip guards would enter and punish us if we were caught talking during our supposedly 'time out for sleep.'

This could be, if I survived, my third year in Burma to witness and experience the forces of nature from the mighty meteorological event in this part of the world: the monster monsoon. I had been exposed to a relatively small part of this event when based in India in 1942 but nothing on the scale that we PoWs experienced in Rangoon. When I sometimes saw massive flashes of lightning and listened to the echoing rolls and roar of thunder during my incarceration, I hoped that there would be a direct strike on our captors. That would have been one of the biggest miracles since the parting of the Dead Sea and yet, a fitting retribution, so I thought at the time, if this were to happen to at least a handful of Japanese.

Another visible sign of changes in the military position of our enemy was confirmed when a number of the regular Japanese prison guards unexpectedly left the gaol. It was rumoured they had been transferred to the battlefronts. There was also a group of about 120 Indian prisoners who had decided to join the Indian National Army and support the Japanese military. What the alternative for these former Indian PoWs was, as far as I recall, never made known to us. Even at this stage of the war, when we knew the Allies were regaining control of Burma, this development evoked something negative in my mind about the dignity and loyalty of at least some of our so-called Indian friends and allies. There were further reports coming to us that the Burmese were also evacuating Rangoon. Some of our Nippon guards, appeared to be drinking alcoholic beverages more than usual and whether this indicated the underlying fear in our captors, and therefore a breakdown in their usually highly disciplined disposition, brought a sense of elation to us, but also apprehension at the unknown outcome of our own safety. There were more visual sightings from our prison of billowing clouds of smoke and explosions. When they were in the north or northeast, we knew the Allies were getting closer to liberating Rangoon. Not once though did the Nips indicate to us what was happening.

One of our fears, which curtailed some of our elation from these developments, were rumours that if the Allies were making steady and successful progress and forcing the Japanese to retreat, then the Japanese authorities might order the execution of every PoW. Given the hardships we were forced to undergo, and the many atrocities already committed by Japanese forces on captured Allies and thousands of civilians throughout South East Asia and the Pacific, these were not unreasonable concerns. When we had to live from one day to the next, not knowing whether we would be alive in five minutes or five days from now, was something most of us wrestled uncomfortably with. Our captors revealed nothing that could be construed as beneficial to our welfare. But we had, if only in our minds, our future to hold onto as free men again. Even more uplifting, in April of 1945, was a delivery of some personal mail to the prisoners, much of which had been held back for at least three years. This was a huge boost to the morale to those prisoners who desperately sought news of their families. In this mail I received several of the postcards that had been forwarded to the Japanese Red Cross posted, it would seem, on a very regular basis by my mother, and from these I gleaned with rapidity the news that my family was still alive; at least from the last dated card.

There were also a number of men coming back from the work parties that had seen several groups of Japanese soldiers and civilians heading out of the city and local Burmese had quietly told them that: 'It won't be long now'. Reports of rioting and looting spread as some essential supplies were now becoming harder to obtain in Rangoon. What quantities of food and other commodities were taken by our Japanese captors can only be guessed at. This indicated to us a breakdown in the supply chain of the Japanese authorities. There also began increased air activity over Burma with greater numbers of American and British fighter and bomber aircraft being spotted. With these came air raids and some massive explosions over Rangoon. The Japanese guards in the prison were seen less and less and, with this development, a diminishing attention to us. Beatings became less frequent also. We now knew that the Allies were winning the war but while this was going on the Nips started to increase the stockpiles of food, wood and other provisions as though they were going to try and hold onto Rangoon and fight the Allies to the last man. With this extra food and fuel entering the gaol, our captors also increased the rations for prisoners.

From around 20 April, and almost every day before we were marched out of Rangoon, our captors were becoming less attentive to us. No working parties were being sent out and several PoWs had witnessed the Nips carrying boxes and bundles of papers (including medical documents it was later revealed) and throwing them onto a bonfire on an open plot of ground in their quarters. We correctly assumed the Japanese were destroying any evidence of their involvement of treatment of their PoWs. By doing this, and with the stockpiling of food and other supplies, then it seemed an evacuation might be imminent. A further reason for this belief was that most of the Japanese in the prison had now changed into what looked like new uniforms. Some men in our prison even suggested that our captors were going to defend Rangoon. We just did not know. It was a very confusing time and I just wanted out.

Rangoon to Pegu and ?

Then it came. We were continually in a state of suspense and additional fears now crept into my debilitated, somewhat skeletal body and frayed nervous system. Toward the last week of April 1945, orders had been given to our prison staff in the provisions storeroom to put together enough food to supply 200 men for at least five days. In reality there were just over 400 of us that finally marched out. This meant our fellow PoWs would be left in limbo. This group of PoWs included several hundred Chinese and Indians, a few Gurkhas and over one hundred British, Commonwealth and American men. The predominantly British, and a few Americans, Australians, Indians and two Ghurkas, if I recall, were 'selected' to be sent on this march. We had been categorised into either 'Fit to walk' or 'Unfit' and promptly divided into two groups. The very ill and physically incapable (the Unfit PoWs), plus a few others who decided to take their chances and remain in Rangoon, were left behind. Those marching out with us included further Air Force prisoners from Block 5. Those who had seen little of the outside of this Block were immensely grateful at this time just to get some fresh air and sunlight. I considered myself fit and able enough to walk and was passed as such.

On 25 April, much of our rations for the intended march had to be loaded into a number of wooden handcarts. These carts were hand pulled and pushed by half a dozen PoWs who would alternate with other prisoners to spread the burden relatively equally. Some pre-cooked rice and soup that had been placed into large buckets for our journey also had to be carried. There were a few wheelbarrows loaded with food and possibly ammunition. Those who could were also forced to carry bags of rice on our heads, shoulders or in our arms. At the same time we were preparing to leave, the Nips were reorganising some of their stockpiled food and storing it in our former compound. Were the Nips intentions to create a subterfuge and con the advancing Allied forces that we had been well cared for or would a siege mentality eventuate? We never found out where our final destination was and the Japanese group leading us as usual gave nothing away.

Under armed guard, we set out along the Rangoon road leading to Pegu, which is roughly north east from Rangoon and approximately fifty miles away. Some of us were given used Japanese military clothes to wear including, shirts, shorts, caps and boots. Despite the somewhat eclectic and incongruous looking appearance of many in this attire, it was a strange sensation, and to me added humiliation, after walking around in either a loin cloth or stitched up, tattered, filthy shorts and bare feet during my incarceration, of now being forced to adorn our bodies with Japanese clothes; a race of people for whom I now nurtured so much enmity. Several of the men who had Nip shoes on ended up discarding them when their feet became very sore and often with blisters forming on heels and toes. In our ration kit we had a few meagre pieces of food including some biscuits. A few of us attached some ration packs to a bamboo pole to carry upon our shoulders and in late afternoon after being lined up by the Nips we began our march from Rangoon. Most of the Nips were walking at the head of our group while three or four guards with loaded rifles and fixed bayonets remained by our sides. Brigadier Hobson, as ever, stood tall and proud and seemed to tower majestically over the Japanese guards when he stood by their side.

On the day we left this 'Hell' called Rangoon Gaol; my 'home' away from home for two gruelling, miserable years, I felt tears and bitterness together. Doctor McLeod, the Canadian doctor and surgeon, remained in Rangoon to look after our fellow PoWs. Some of us had also written short letters, which would hopefully be forwarded to our families if we did not survive this march. Several of us turned round for a quick last view of the prison as we walked out of the gate, which closed immediately after our exit. Two years ago I had been taken through this very same gate into another world and existence. God, how I hated the Japanese.

We quietly talked amongst ourselves at this point. So many memories of the horrors that had been committed, and possibly more for those still imprisoned, crowded my mind. When one door closes another opens; so the saying goes. Once out of Rangoon, and walking on the road to Pegu, the jungle vegetation became increasingly dense. We were forced to march throughout the night and stopped for a few hours rest on the morning of 26 April. This day was harder than ever and several men were already near exhaustion. Even though we were supposed to be relatively fit for Japanese PoWs, there were men on this march who were visibly very ill. Though we were all emaciated to some extent, I was not optimistic for several of our men surviving long. We had some rain on this part of the march but it was nothing to the monsoon downpours I had experienced.

During this early part of our walk, one PoW was left at the side of the road after collapsing and the guards ordered us to keep going. It was very likely that the Jap guards bayoneted this poor soul as they often did to prisoners who collapsed from exhaustion or illness. It was on the third day of our march when we realised why the Nips may have given us some of their clothing to wear. An Allied Mosquito aircraft must have spotted us and mistakenly taken us to be Japanese soldiers; it dropped one bomb which landed close by. This landed behind us as we scrambled for cover into the side of the road. While it was uplifting to view Allied aircraft increasingly gain superiority of air space over Burma, the unknowns of our future hammered away at us.

Most of us immediately discarded the Nips clothes despite the apparent curses by some of the armed sentries nearby. Strangely enough no prisoners were beaten for this action. The Nips wanted to keep us alive, but possibly as some form of leverage for their own survival. We took small amounts of our rationed food at each break and most meals, when we could cook it, still consisted of rice. We prisoners had no conception of our fate, nor that of our comrades left behind in Rangoon Gaol. The bags of rice we were forced to carry, some of which weighed as much as 20 lbs, were passed around on a rotational system. Given the poor physical condition our bodies were in we did this approximately every thirty minutes.

Our march continued on the same road to Pegu and as we made our way, we encountered a number of trucks and cars with Japanese Soldiers and the Indian National Army, also heading away from Rangoon. Along this road there were several unexpected attacks by Allied fighter planes, obviously thinking we were part of the Japanese forces, and when they flew in low to attack we all moved as fast as possible, some of us helping those who were struggling, and headed for shelter behind trees or into ditches, anything that would provide immediate protection for us. There were some houses, most looked deserted, and woodlands on either side of our march while heading into Pegu.

It was on the 28 April that we entered near Pegu, which had been badly damaged from earlier air raids and possible ground exchanges of fighting. Pegu had, in fact, been bombed by 99 Squadron approximately two years ago on one of our sorties. On reaching Pegu we then crossed a bridge, which the Nips destroyed shortly after our crossing. From here we ended up on a railway line. By now our handcarts were left behind with some of what little food we had. The walk along the railway lines was slow and agonising because at times some of us accidentally missed the sleepers and trod on the rocks, which caused cuts to our feet. We left the railway line on the night of the twenty-eighth and took to walking on a bullock track, which was less painful to traverse. We had not walked these distances before and April was one of the hottest times of the year. The exhaustion bit deeper and harder. Many men used bamboo poles for support and to keep them upright. Some of the fitter men could be seen supporting a fellow PoW as we trudged along.

While incarcerated in Rangoon, most of us obviously contemplated if and when our suffering would end. As we marched, word gradually passed among us that, of the 400 of us who left Rangoon Gaol, a few (including Australians) had managed to escape into the jungle. How many I do not know, for I never heard of their fate. Doctor MacKenzie was now also in a critical condition. His beriberi had markedly deteriorated and he had to be assisted by fellow prisoners for some miles. At this point, he could not stand without support. Because of his critical state, Doctor MacKenzie, had been sitting inside a cart for part of the journey to Pegu, and the conscience of the Japanese guards in allowing this was exceptional to my thinking. Our doctors were held in high esteem by every inmate, and maybe even by some of our Nip guards. It was around this time word quickly spread that Doctor MacKenzie had requested a Japanese guard or officer to end his life by shooting him through the heart. Fortunately, this did not occur and two PoWs, Hansell and Martin, both Sergeants, found in their constitution strength enough to carry our great doctor to our yet unknown destination. I thought this might have been Siam (now Thailand).

Chapter 6

1945: Liberation

On the morning of Sunday 29 April, we stopped at a village on the Pegu-Wau Road. O'Hari San, one of the senior Nippon Officers who had marched with us from Rangoon Gaol, was asked to provide assistance to Doctor MacKenzie. O'Hari San walked away and a short time later Brigadier Hobson came out from the village hut he had been in. With an ecstatic voice, and standing in front of us, our Brigadier asked for our attention and then spoke with a clear, firm and emotional voice; 'Men, we are free, we are free; or words to that effect.' The silver lining was at hand.

It is hard to describe and recall my innermost feelings at this precise moment. Here we sat, crouched, or stood, some of us slightly perplexed and huddled together like cattle in a yard. We were approximately 400 men and now ex-prisoners of the Japanese; most overwhelmingly exhausted, generally skeletal and of a ragged and dirty appearance. Our march had been another punishing experience. Dressed in filthy pieces of clothing, starving and in dire need of fluids, many men required urgent medical attendance if they were going to live. In this circumstance, we were told we were emancipated men. Not prisoners, but men of liberty. While we all understood these words, it seemed to me, given our condition, as though the absolutely unexpected and opposite situation was outside my orbit of punishment, pain and suffering that mingled hazily with my exhausted thinking. As Hobson repeated these words many men were in tears, others inwardly contemplating and gazing in a blank, deep hush while some were hollering with ecstatic cries of rapture.

The feeling of being physically and emotionally liberated would take some time to come to terms with.

It was not until we witnessed the last of the Nip guards actually walking out of the village, and then out of our sight, which was remarkably soon after our Brigadier's announcement, that for the first time since our capture we were possibly now alone. Our immediate morale and elation rose significantly. Can you imagine the jubilation of this news and the sight of watching the backs of our despised tyrants leave without physically harming us? At the very least many of us expected to be either executed or severely beaten prior to the Nips retreat. O'Hari San and the Commandant had been informed by Hobson that his men were to return to Rangoon immediately. Obviously things were going very badly for the Japanese war machine. As soon as the Nips had left the area, some of our physically able ex-PoWs set out to locate a nearby village, one of dozens along our long march, to try and obtain food and basic medical supplies. This did not take long and the Burmese locals who were relatively close by in the next village were helpful to some extent. This first meal we were able to eat without the presence of any Japanese guard lurking nearby was one of the most enjoyable moments of our lives since incarceration. Many of us still panicked and looked around every time we heard a strange noise thinking we might be beaten or attacked yet by our foe. Paranoia, death and disease were still as one with us while we resided in Burma. We remained in this village as preparations were made to contact Allied headquarters. Approximately two hours after this most wonderful change in our circumstances, there was a sudden volley of shouting from several of our men that Allied fighter planes were zeroing in on us; no doubt in the belief that we were part of a Japanese convoy. Panic spread as men called out to those around them. We scrambled for cover. Some of the men headed for the huts and others, including myself, moved onto one side of the road into ditches, holes or took cover within some of the vegetation. We heard and felt several explosions of gunfire from the strafing unnervingly close to us with fragments of debris scattering around. Volleys of machine gun sprays from Spitfires screamed through the air. A few seconds later, we observed these aircraft flying in low towards the village and I huddled with my knees drawn up to my chest behind a tree trunk until all fighters flew off. My nervous system was already severely damaged and I have reflected many times how much more of a 'beating' my body could have endured.

Several minutes after taking cover, we emerged into the open again and all seemed quiet. We looked at the damage and sought to get medical aid to a number of injured men. Several of our fellow men died in this attack and several were wounded. While this was happening a Captain from our group emerged from one of the huts, badly shaken up, and in a stressed voice, called for our attention. He informed us that Brigadier Hobson had been fatally shot by a bullet from one of the Spitfires. Hobson had died almost immediately. The silence, mingled with a sense of fear, when this announcement was given was followed by able men quietly moving about doing what we could to assist those in most need of aid.

Another day of sorrow and a tragic end to our Brigadier; a great man who had endured over three and a half years as a PoW in Rangoon only to end his final moments just shortly after being freed by the Japanese. The irony of it all has been something I have contemplated numerous times in the years following the war. Our one consolation during this moment was that our Brigadier had been able to see, and sense, the joy of his victorious announcement. Later in the day, and after most of us had moved on to another village, a grave was dug and a lugubrious ceremony was conducted by those few whom it had been decided should remain behind to give final respects to Brigadier Hobson; a friend who had always shown great fortitude and kindness to every prisoner he had contact with.

Following this raid it was decided to try and signal to any further Allied aircraft in the area of our new location by placing some white cloth torn into pieces to form an SOS in large letters. This was in addition to highlighting the words that British PoWs were located here. These signals were eventually picked up by an Allied fighter plane and position details of our group we felt assured would be relayed to Headquarters. We could hear explosions, at various interludes, to the north and north east of us and we assumed these were allied forces engaging with Japanese and Indian National Army forces. At the same time we relocated to another nearby village, inhabited by this time friendly Burmese, considering my earlier experiences with them I was not so easily put at ease. However we were well fed and looked forward to a relatively peaceful night. We were not here long before being instructed to head back to the village where our Brigadier had died.

Major Lutz and a couple of others volunteered, including myself, to inform troops of part of the Allied 14th Army to stop bombing the village where the remaining ex-PoWs were still sheltering. We went willingly, and after a relatively short time met up with a group of West Yorks and Ghurkas, to whom we passed information to regarding the village. A Major in a Bren Carrier was in charge, immediately detailed our fellow servicemen's position and contacted 48 Brigade Headquarters, which were located at Kadok. This is where I stayed until we were finally picked up by our own transport. We were informed at this time that Germany was facing imminent collapse, and that the Allies were nearing the final days of retaking Burma. This news was of enormous magnitude, because we former prisoners had been kept virtually completely ignorant of the Allies victories, of battles fought or lost. News like this further allayed our fear of the Japanese, the Indian Nationalist Army and their Burmese supporters as a viable enemy. That was the end of our incarceration by the Japanese Imperial Forces by my reckoning. Our long, grim days and nights were hopefully over. The twenty-ninth day of April is, like several other momentous occasions, forever etched into my mind.

Eripe me de inimicis (Deliver me from mine enemies)

Now liberated men, we were finally transported in the backs of lorries, the critically ill, including Doctor MacKenzie went in an ambulance, to a field hospital station some miles further on which became the first point of our rehabilitation. Stationed here was part of the West Yorkshire Regiment. What the medical and military personnel thought as we climbed out of this transport must have been something of a shock to their senses when we revealed our severely malnourished and dehydrated bodies. Many of us had open sores and infected cuts, nearly all bare footed and covered in grime and dirt. We were immediately given food, fluids and Red Cross supplies plus additional items of clothing, a medical check and initial treatment to wounds. After living in such wretched, squalid conditions, and being deprived of the most basic of necessities, these personal items brought some of us to tears.

To many people in the world today, the change in our circumstances may seem hard to visualise in their minds. For many months afterwards, the sensation of holding in my hands a most basic commodity like a comb or hair brush to tidy my hair was such a wonderful feeling. For the first time in over two years I could sleep in a bed with linen, have a wash with clean hot water and soap, use a toothbrush and toothpaste, a razor and blade, and toilet paper along with a set of fresh, spotless new clothes, fresh food on plates with cutlery, a handkerchief and other items. The taste of a plate covered with western food was like ambrosia. To drink a cup of tea with milk and even a small quantity of sugar was nectar to our taste buds. For many weeks after liberation when meals were given to us,

I sometimes considered whether I should retain a portion for later consumption; such was the thinking in my mind after experiencing a prolonged period of chronic hunger and the consequences of a starvation diet. Accepting these new and changed circumstances was not easy to accustom myself with. To readjust our lives accordingly, to know that we had not been forsaken and were now emancipated men, would take some of us much longer to settle into.

My stomach and bowels were in a delicate condition and I could only consume very small quantities of light food at this stage. A couple of days later we were transferred to India to a British General Hospital where further medical checks were done on every former PoW. As far as I know, we were all suffering to varying degree with beriberi as well as numerous other problems like tropical ulcers. Part of our immediate rehabilitation was for every former PoW to be fed food of high nutritional content in an effort to rebuild our atrophied bodies including as much Vitamin B as possible to fight beriberi. This diet included some dairy products, fruit and juices and even beer. We were given Mepacrine tablets to combat the effects of Malaria. We were given copies of newspapers and magazines to reengage our minds and come to terms with the events in the world of which we knew nothing during our incarceration. How we talked, laughed and sometimes cried among ourselves well into many nights and throughout the days of this convalescence at the military messes and local hotels. We had a chance to talk to several members of the press and military intelligence personnel who, in disbelief, recorded our experiences as Prisoners of War of the Japanese. I wondered how much the politics of the present and near future would determine what the public in Allied nations would ever know of what we PoWs went through.

I felt though, as the days progressed and my health gradually made headway, my emotions were torn betwixt memories of the multitudinous horrors of the preceding two years, and a hankering to extricate myself from India and return home to Great Britain. I could not feel a complete deliverance from our enemy nor engender an internal sense of ease. The fact was that my nerves were in such a debilitated condition, and the raw memories of the past two years were rigidly fixed in my thinking for many hours each day and night. Partly because of this I felt too uncomfortably near Burma, and the Japanese were not so far away in my mind either; so my fears remained. This invisible trepidation and the daily reminder of visible scars about my body from torture and jungle sores exacerbated these feelings. I reflected often on the loss of my close friend Paul Griffiths but had to be grateful that I, and many others, survived to live on. After several weeks of round-the-clock care, ample food, rest, medical checks and a standard of hygiene that we former PoWs revelled in, my time in this part of the world was nearing its end. In India, we were treated with great kindness by all.

News came through that our fellow PoWs left behind in Rangoon Gaol at the time of our march out to just north of Pegu, a distance of approximately 70 miles we were informed, had been found alive. Two short letters had been written in English and left in Rangoon Gaol by the now fleeing Japanese forces as they retreated from Burma. One of these was attached to the main gate of Rangoon Gaol and dated 29 April 1945. It read:

To the whole captured persons of Rangoon Gaol. According to the Nippon military order, we hereby give you liberty and admit to leave this place at your own will. Regarding food and other materials kept in the compound, we give you permission to consume them, as far as your necessity is concerned. We hope that we shall have an opportunity to meet you again at battlefield of somewhere. We shall continue our war effort eternally in order to get the emancipation of all Asiatic races.

Haruo Ito
Chief Officer of Rangoon Branch Gaol.

The Japanese had deserted Rangoon Gaol on 29 April, so at the time the Allies had their troops on the ground and entered Rangoon, the expected heavy fighting between the belligerents never materialised. Fortunately this episode became a 'bloodless' emancipation for the remaining PoWs in the prison.

For many of us, our thoughts now tended more and more to dwell on our homes, family and friends. How I longed to be able to walk into 10, Kirby Road again and talk to my mother, father, brother and three sisters and see the looks on their faces. After two years of not having any contact with them I received a telegram from home after first sending my own message via Red Cross channels who gave priority to inform all relatives of our situation following our release by the Japanese. I knew now they had all survived the war. I had already decided, while recuperating in India, to surprise my family by arriving several weeks earlier than was anticipated in my initial correspondence. The war was still going on in parts of South East Asia and the Pacific but my understanding was that the Japanese were being routed on every battlefront and the Allies were in control of the inevitable outcome.

Of great significance and further positive news was the announcement on 7 May that the war in Europe was over following Germany's surrender. This is remembered as VE Day and there were wild celebrations around the world, yet in this part of South East Asia, the Allies were still fighting the Japanese and the now scattered remnants of their supporters. It seemed a little strange that the war had ended in Europe. So many images and thoughts of this very recent past, of the consequences from the destruction wrought by belligerents on both sides of this conflict, encompassed my mind. News of the vast areas of devastation wrought on cities and towns throughout Europe and Great Britain during the final years of the war, which I had not been directly involved in for over two years were, at times, incomprehensible to many of us. Any and every piece of information we could obtain, denied us inside Rangoon Gaol, was devoured with rapidity. The massive air raids over Germany, and the Normandy Campaign which I later found out my brother Bob was part of, captivated our attention. On one end of the scale I felt relief and unbridled joy at our changed circumstances. At the other end was the future; the unknown. Nothing could prepare many returning service personnel and civilians for their homecoming to Britain, Europe and elsewhere with this magnitude of loss and destruction and the many inevitable changes to our lives. One thing we did know with absolute certainty: our incarceration had changed us immeasurably.

I was informed a couple of weeks later following our transfer to India that on the other side of the world, commencing on 29 April and the same day of our liberation, was the beginning of Operation Manna over Western Holland; Germany's persecution of Holland had included food blockades and resulted in much suffering. The Dutch people were so short of food that around 20,000 of its citizens died from starvation and hundreds of thousands were malnourished. The RAF had begun flights to drop around 7,000 tons of food aid principally by Lancaster Bombers, which was then augmented by American aircraft. The coincidence of these events is ever present whenever I recall this day.

Part III

Chapter 7

1945: Horsell; Here I Come

In May 1945 a telegram arrived from the British War Office advising the Tate family that I had been found alive in Burma after liberation by the Allies and would, as soon as formalities were finalised and passed as medically fit, be transported home. This was the news my family had desperately been waiting for: to know that I was still alive. There were moments when the worst had been feared. Fear, anguish and the aggregated years of exhaustion from this war, compounded by the 'unknown' of their eldest son began to partly dissipate. The feeling of immense joy and tears of relief that I was not only alive, but could be expected to return to England within a few months instilled a new energy and long-lost optimism into my family.

My father was at work when the telegram arrived. Irene, the youngest of my siblings was at home with mother and was sent to tell father that I was alive. Irene, aged 16 at the time, seemed like she was in a panic when she found father and said to him, in tears: 'It's Bill.' My father thought it was grim news and, yelling at Irene, asked: 'What's happened?' Irene replied: 'Bill's alive.' Father, by then employed in the Printing Department of Vickers Armstrong at Brooklands, immediately left work and hurried home with Irene to read the telegram. Ivy, the eldest of my three sisters, was also at work at the Woking Co-Operative. Father and Mother went to her workplace with the news of Bill. Equally important, and of great urgency, was that I could also forward a letter home to them, assuming that they were alive as well, to let them know of my circumstances and was free of the 'HELL' I had been forced to go through.

The war had caused the health of many people throughout the world to suffer. Very few citizens in Britain were immune from the hardships, loss and sacrifices. The physical and emotional toll on my mother was clearly visible. Both my mother and father had aged much over those six years. As well as wartime rationing, air raids and the constant worry for her family and friends, the stress of two sons having to fight was perhaps the hardest situation to come to terms with. Mother had suffered tremendously from two years of uncertainty regarding my circumstances. My mother, father, brother and sisters, naturally worried about what may or may not have become of me; what I was doing if alive, and wondering if I would ever return home after being listed as missing in Burma. Naturally my mother and father had fought to maintain a spirit of hope and unyielding faith of better times ahead. I am sure that most people of today's generation cannot even imagine the day-to-day stress and anxiety of those war years.

On 15 of June 1945 I flew out of India in a Dakota airplane with other former PoWs. What an exhilarating and immense feeling of relief at that moment when our plane finally lifted off the runway and headed skywards; back to my home and country. After the dozens of missions I had flown over Europe and Burma in Wellingtons I still relished the joy of flight again. We had a couple of short stopovers on the return journey and, after fifty hours in the air, we landed in England amidst a roar of exultation from everyone in the plane. It was a day I will never forget. To feel my body on home soil again in an English speaking country was another emotional moment for us. I had to re-engage for a short period with some RAF personnel. I had further discussions and was also provided with a new uniform. I was given immediate and extended leave. I needed time and space to think through the teeming emotional turmoil of my mind.

On the day of my return to Horsell, my sister Ivy was chatting to Mrs Brownjohn, one of our neighbours. Mrs Brownjohn suddenly remarked to Ivy: 'that's your Billy coming up the road.' Ivy replied to Mrs Brownjohn that 'Bill is still in the Air Force and not yet expected home.' As Ivy turned she saw a somewhat tall, thin looking man approaching, and walking in a rather casual manner along Kirby Road wearing a khaki coloured uniform. I was wearing what looked like a felt bush hat with a wide rim. This was part of an outfit that I was given after liberation. Although having been issued with a new RAF uniform I decided to surprise my family by changing into the gear issued when in India.

Not being dressed in my RAF uniform, this left Ivy unsure for several seconds at the stranger she was staring at, and had to calm her racing mind. As I walked closer, my much thinner facial features revealed themselves to Ivy. The reality struck home as she finally recognised her 'big' brother. Ivy was simultaneously overcome with rapture and disbelief at seeing me after everything that had occurred during nearly six years of war. Ivy ran up the road to me and gave me a hug, breaking into tears after finally seeing me alive and home again, amid the family's past fears.

What most of the family did not or could not comprehend, nor did I for that matter, was the psychological damage I was perennially scarred with. Many of these PoW experiences had now become permanent and inseparable additions to my personality. They were intangible components attached to my pre-war experiences and of what remained of my life. How could they ever not be so? On my return to England I was still relatively emaciated. My much-changed physical looks were very noticeable to family, friends and neighbours who had remembered me prior to my time as a PoW. They were all wonderfully sympathetic, and encouraged me continually with their kind thoughts. All former PoWs had been instructed to assiduously follow a diet of regular nutritious food and adequate rest along the lines of our initial rehabilitation in India. The colour of my skin had also turned a shade yellow as a result of the *Mepacrine* tablets I was taking for malaria. Many former PoWs, including myself, were assigned to travel by boat back to England as part of our gradual recuperation. Like every other former PoW however, I needed to return home to family and friends and immerse myself with familiar surroundings by getting as far away from Burma and Japan, with all its attendant hellish memories and experiences, as soon as possible.

My 'baby' sister Irene, now a teenager, was outside the front of the house and when she noticed me holding Ivy, I called out to her and said: 'hello little sister; remember me?' Irene ran inside to tell my mother and father I was home. Although my return had been anticipated, the emotional reaction of my parents as they saw me walk into their home again was something I shall never forget. My mother was in tears as her pent up torment melted when she embraced me. The one member of the family not at home was Bob, who was still on active service in Singapore. When Bob finally returned from Singapore in late 1945 the family was reunited again for the first time in six years.

One of my cousins, Dolly (Stoker) recalled the moment when news of my safe return from Burma was received up north in County Durham. My dear Aunt Edie (Stoker) Pratt and Uncle Les (Stoker), my mother's siblings, said that they had never given up hope for my survival. I recalled many times over the years, with great sentiment, of my leave entitlements during the war with my 'Geordie' relatives in Houghton-le-Spring, County Durham. Uncle Les, his wife Mary and their children would occasionally visit my parents for a holiday after the war. My kindly Uncle Les had been a coal miner all his working life and had worked in the Ryhope, Shotton and Silksworth collieries. At one time, Uncle Les had been Secretary of the Miners Union at the Ryhope Lodge; he sadly died from *pneumonicosis* in 1981, the result from years of inhalation of coal dust.

A few days after my return home a street party was being organised for me as my family and neighbours in Kirby Road wished to show their concern and support to me for my 'lost time.' Before this celebration however, I had a promise to keep that I had made to my superiors in Rangoon Gaol. I now sought out Paul Griffiths family. This promise of mine would be difficult to fulfil. Knowing Paul's parents would be distraught, I wanted to be able to provide as much information to them as possible, though I deliberately censored some of the more gruesome situations experienced by PoWs, in the hope that the death of their son could somehow be made a little less traumatic. What can you say to the parents of a son who had been buried in a cemetery on the other side of the world in the Far East? I told them that Paul and I had flown together in 99 Squadron. Recounting my experience in the Wellington Paul and I had flown in for the last time, I gave as much detail as I could of our last sortie prior to bailing out. I left Paul's family with much sorrow.

The street party in my honour was a wonderful occasion. Neighbours along Kirby Road helped set up tables in the street and, because rationing was still in force, each household contributed what they could of food and drinks for the party. Two poles had been erected and a banner attached to it with the message 'Welcome Home Bill' outside No 10, Kirby Road. This was a wonderful day in my life. Although I knew I was safe in England and would not suffer any further violence at the hands of the Japanese, not a day went by without cogitations of my experiences of this war. Apart from the daily reports from around the world of 'mopping up' exercises by Allied forces, my detestation for the Japanese was a seemingly insurmountable barrier to try and erase from my mind.

Lasting Effects

For nearly five years following my return from Burma, I was constantly paranoid of any one walking behind me who happened to be wearing soft-soled rubber shoes or boots and had to continually turn round to see who was there. This specific sound immediately rekindled flashbacks of the time I was imprisoned in Rangoon Gaol. Mentioning this now causes me to recall a particular incident as a PoW in Compound 3. At the time I was trying to locate an army Private who wished to speak to me. As I was walking through the compound I heard a Nip guard quietly pattering up behind me. I stopped and turned round to face him as he approached. I immediately bowed to him in the Japanese fashion; as I had done so hundreds of times in the past to avoid a beating. The guard immediately yelled at me, '*Kiotsuke?*' ('Where go?') I said that I needed to see an Army prisoner. The guard replied: 'He no good?' To which I answered in English: 'Yes, he good.' The guard apparently did not tolerate or accept my reply, possibly because he thought I simply contradicted his statement. Or perhaps he just decided to wreak further injury upon me for the sake of some personal satisfaction and indifference. I would never know, because he suddenly lashed out at me with one of his boots and started to kick me on the outside of my left leg. He then punched the left and right sides of my face with a clenched fist and after this episode he simply walked away. I do not know to this day why that particular beating remains with me after the much worse experiences I had suffered at the hands of the Honourable Japanese Imperial Forces.

Since flying home I had been waking up some nights terrified, sweating and occasionally screaming. Images of beatings, torture, starvation, the inside of the gaol, and Japanese guards remained with me; not forgetting either the deaths of some Allied servicemen in Rangoon Gaol. In an attempt to curb these nightmares, and feeling embarrassed at waking other family members in the night, I forced myself to stay awake so as not to disturb anyone. This sleep deprivation, a part of my life since first joining the RAF, was to become very much the norm for the remainder of my life. There were many nights at this juncture when particular sounds, even the slightest rustling, would have me wide awake and scrambling virtually instantaneously out of my bed in fright and looking to see if a Japanese guard was nearby. On these occasions I sometimes went and rechecked all the locks in the house; windows and doors included until I was satisfied in my mind of being safe. More than once other members of the family, that I had unintentionally woken, came out to see what I was doing, unable to comprehend my 'strange' behaviour.

To overcome these night time disturbances, and after my parents being unable to find a solution to my acute anxiety, I visited the family's local doctor, more than once over the next few weeks, to seek advice on appropriate treatment. Sleeping pills were prescribed, regular exercise and most importantly a recommendation to keep my mental faculties focused on activities other than the war. The last of these was impossible to achieve at this point. While on leave there were some days when I also drank, initially because of my damaged and delicate nervous system. Alcohol was one solution to try and cope with each day as my recent experiences and memories so vividly played in my mind. Some of my own family did not, or could not, understand yet the condition of my body. It was during some of these occasions when I would 'open up' to a few people, including fellow RAF personnel, and my mother and father, who kept prodding me to tell them about the experiences I and other PoWs suffered during our captivity. My father, probably more than anyone else, understood some of these problems because of his own experiences during the First World War on the Western Front.

However, it remained very difficult to reveal this past to family and close friends. Sometimes I related to them parts of my ordeals;

most I could not. I don't know why. I later thought that, because many experiences were of such a macabre and sinister nature, I would cause too much anguish to my family and friends had they known more of what I had witnessed, and suffered, every day for two years in Rangoon Gaol. Some experiences were also too humiliating, in my mind, to talk about. For many years, I maintained a mostly guarded dialogue when the subject was broached. There were moments of reflection when I wondered if I would ever be able to live even a relatively 'normal' life. Upon returning to England we had no counselling of any sort by a Psychiatrist or Psychologist. If we were passed as being medically fit physically, our psychological considerations were seemingly never paramount and this is one of the primary reasons why so many former PoWs suffered breakdowns as the years passed. The authorities did not consider it plausible that we should harbour internal 'demons' from our recent tribulations.

Third, there were occasions when even a knock at the door would have me suddenly 'escaping' to another room in a terror-stricken frame of mind to hide and not be noticed. I could not, at this time, comprehend my feelings of heightened fear and panic when I was now safe at home in England. My mother and father always reassured me that I was safe and the Japanese could not, and would not harm me again. Some habits, it would seem, are hard to disencumber oneself from. But the worst of these experiences remained a 'Closed Shop' in my mind. I could not tell anyone at that point in time.

It was the dropping of two atomic bombs on Hiroshima and Nagasaki in August 1945 that would compel the Emperor of Japan to order Japanese forces to surrender and finally end the war. Like most people at the time, I had no idea of what this new weapon, the atomic bomb, actually was, or its destructive capabilities. This weapon was being made known to the masses for the first time. My first reaction, from the photographs I later saw of the devastation, was that the Japanese people were, rightly or wrongly, being punished for some of the suffering and loss that thousands of Allied service personnel and civilians throughout their incursions had been subjected to. Although the Second World War may have been brought to a conclusion more quickly through the deployment of atomic bombs, the debate over this decision still rages today. Finally, I knew that these new and powerful weapons had forever changed the rules and outcomes of future conflicts; whether used as a deterrent, or as a threat. My fascination for aircraft would remain a lifetime passion for me. This was one of the reasons I regularly attended military and civilian air shows, when possible, throughout my life.

After several months of service-leave and slowly, but gradually, regaining the much-needed weight I had lost as a PoW, I felt capable of re-engaging in duties with the RAF, even though the condition of my nervous system was questionable. I needed to keep my mind occupied as much as possible upon instructions from my doctor. Taking prescribed sleeping pills, which helped to reduce the nightmares, and being back on active duty, allowed me to talk with many other returned servicemen of our wartime experiences. What tremendous discussions they were, often tinged with sadness at the revelations of personal experiences that many of us hadn't realised had occurred to other service personnel and ordinary citizens. Many long evenings were spent talking over the minute details of the war. Six long years of fighting were now over. Six very long years, and so much of the world we had known in 1939 had gone, or changed forever.

As I was still in the RAF, and had not decided on a definite plan for my future, I was posted to RAF Bases Farnborough and Melksham. By December 1945, I was officially promoted to the rank of Warrant Officer. Following my first Christmas at home with family since 1941, and a most wonderful time for me, I still managed to receive additional days of leave from my RAF duties due to my health. In early 1946, I was posted to No 7 Flight Instructor

School to undertake further courses and training. I had considered staying on in the RAF to pursue a career post-war, but possibly in administration only; I had witnessed and endured enough of combat duty. I also had my own inner demons to contend with yet, and I did not relish the thought of ever again having to experience active hostilities against another country and its citizens.

Chapter 8

1946: Resigning from the RAF

In early 1946 something very wonderful and unforeseen happened to me that would result in a complete change in my life, thoughts and aspirations. I began my courtship with Irene (Rene) Cox. I had met Rene on a couple of occasions when I was home in Horsell during the last half of 1945, she worked with my sister Ivy at the Woking Co-operative and they were close friends. Rene was, to me, a most beautiful and vivacious 20-year-old lass and I was enchanted with her. It was the beginning of 1946 however, before any serious relationship started.

The annual Woking Fair took place on Wheatsheaf Common in Woking and had been a local attraction for many years. Rene, Ivy and I had agreed to spend the day together at the fair and it was on this day that I asked Rene if she would go out with me. She agreed and we met for our first date the following Saturday evening at a local cinema, the Ritz, in Woking.

Prior to courting me, Rene had been dating a soldier by the name of George, who was still serving in the Coldstream Guards and, like myself, hailed from County Durham. When Rene and I began to see each other on a regular basis, she wrote a 'Dear John' letter (the term given to correspondence from one person to another during the war when you wanted to end a relationship) explaining to George as delicately as she could that she was no longer interested in him and was dating someone else. George wrote a rather caustic letter of reply, which she discarded and set her sights on her future with me.

As my thoughts became increasingly dominated with spending as much time with Rene as possible, I actually committed a breach of duty, which resulted in my receiving a severe reprimand from my superiors. While my rank of Warrant Officer was not affected, I felt that I could not cope with any more stress and did not want to have to explain to my Commanding Officer in detail the experiences I had suffered at the hands of the Japanese. I felt they would not have considered this reason as acceptable for my behaviour, nor was it within their range of responsibilities. These memories of my time as a PoW even affected my ability to settle into a regular day-to-day work pattern. One of the problems was a sensation of claustrophobia and the need to be outdoors as much as possible. With this temperament I had decided that enough was enough. I therefore gave notice of my service to stay in the RAF. In one sense I felt much sadness at severing ties with this crucial part of my life, but inwardly I knew it was the right time to seek another career and lifestyle. After my resignation I wanted to marry the love of my life: Rene.

On several occasions during 1946, prior to our marriage, Rene and I, along with two friends of hers, Lee Smithers and Daphne Guyett, would take day trips out of Woking. If the weather was fine, we sometimes rode our pushbikes about seven miles to Guildford, and spent several hours punting on the river or canal. For those who might not be familiar with Punting as a mode of transport, a Punt is a narrow, flat-bottomed boat that is propelled by a pole controlled by the punter. Our little group would make a day of it, slowly moving our way through the peaceful and slow-flowing waterways in that part of Surrey. I would do the punting and at some point on the journey, while discussing many and varied topics, we would usually sing our favourite songs that had been popular throughout the 1930s and 40s. When we stopped for a break on the canal bank I occasionally recalled, during these moments of inner calm and happiness, a few lines from one of Thomas Hardy's poems entitled *Best Times.*

> *We went a day's excursion to the stream,*
> *Basked by the bank, and bent to the ripplegleam,*
> *And I did not know*
> *That life would show,*
> *However it may flower, no finer glow.*

I am reminded of another elevated moment of bliss and harmony during an excursion to Guildford on our trusty pushbikes. Just before we came into Guildford itself, there was a hill and as we approached the top, we all started singing *Oh, What a Beautiful Mornin'* at the tops of our voices and in unison. Another of Rene and Lee's favourite songs, '*Peg O' My Heart*', usually found its way into our repertoire. When we arrived at Guildford we usually chained our bikes up on the bank of the canal before setting off in the punt. After an hour or two we would find a nice location to relax and enjoy our picnic lunch of tea, lemonade, homemade cakes and sandwiches. At the afternoon's end, and if we were too tired to cycle home, we would catch a train home from nearby Guildford Railway Station.

As romances bloomed and thoughts of the war were gradually replaced with plans for the future, Ivy Tate, Rene Cox, Lee Lord and Daphne Guyett, 'The Kirby Road Girls', as they jokingly called themselves throughout the war years when they attended local dances, were now four young women who would see each other as a group less frequently. These close friends, who had been through so many highs and lows, particularly during the war years, were all on the cusp of new directions and destinations in their journey of life. There would be marriages and children, and some unforeseen tragedies, yet almost always interwoven with hope for a better future and some of the joys of life, whether planned or not.

About eight months following the end of the war, tragedy befell the Tate family just when we thought some semblance of normality was returning to our lives. In early April of 1946 the chronic duodenal ulcer that my father had suffered with for many years perforated. William was very ill and in great pain, and was admitted into Woking's Victoria Cottage Hospital until he was stabilised. He was then transferred to Botleys Park War Hospital in Chertsey, Surrey. Botleys Park War Hospital was a converted eighteenth century mansion and had been founded as a 'colony for mental defectives' in 1932 by Surrey County Council after other institutions in the district became overcrowded. During the Second World War the hospital was used as a war hospital staffed by doctors and nurses from St Thomas's Hospital in London. Patients came from London hospitals evacuated during the Blitz, including wounded servicemen and women from Dunkirk and the D-Day Landings. Following the bombing of the Vickers Armstrong Aircraft factory in nearby Weybridge, injured civilians were also treated here during the war. Botleys Park eventually became part of St Peter's Hospital when control was transferred to the National Health Service in 1948.

My father survived the operation and was considered well enough to return home on Monday 15 April. We had visited him on Sunday, 14 April, a relatively warm day, and the family spent several hours together. Early the next morning, my mother received a house visit from one of the hospital staff and was told that William had passed away. A pulmonary embolus (obstruction of an artery by a blood clot) had formed which had resulted in a heart attack. He had returned to his ward bed after showering and was about to have a cup of tea prior to collecting his personal belongings when he suffered his heart attack. William was just 49 years old. Coming so soon after the war, and with the family again reunited, was a huge setback after everything we had been through since 1939.

My father's funeral service and burial took place at St Mary's Church in Horsell, being the Tate family's house of worship since moving to Woking. The service was a small affair with family and some of William's friends present. Elizabeth bore her sadness and loss as best she could and, with Bill, Bob, Esther and Irene still living at home, the family slowly moved forward. I recall taking my sister Ivy to see our father at the funeral parlour prior to the funeral. I had seen so many ill and dying men and I talked to Ivy of the losses we all have to face from time to time: 'life goes on and we have to try and get on with it.' I occasionally reflected on my own life and wondered why so many of the experiences that had the greatest impact on my life, both tragedies and joyous occasions in the Tate family, occurred ironically, or seemed it seemed, in the months of April and November. The number thirteen also was of significance to me. I was born in April, became a PoW in April and was liberated in April. My father also passed away in April. Rene and I were married on 13 November and the house we first called our own was No 13.

While trying to support and comfort my mother after father's death, much of the responsibility to help the family recover from this loss and cope with future needs fell primarily to me. This did not unduly bother me at this stage. I was earning a reasonable salary and I had already experienced and witnessed much tragedy and hardship. I just hoped that I would make sensible decisions. Rene and I continued to see each other more frequently so when, a few weeks later, my sister Ivy and husband Tony were planning to go to Ventnor on the Isle of Wight for the weekend, they invited Rene (chaperoned by Ivy), and I to go with them. My father and mother had several times taken our family of seven for holidays to the Isle of Wight prior to the war. It was always a pleasure to be able to spend time on this beautiful Isle. Tony, Ivy, Rene and I travelled by train to Portsmouth and then boarded a ferry for the journey from Portsmouth to Ryde on the Isle of Wight.

Mrs Nune, the landlady whom our family had always stayed with prior to the war, had kept her coastal holiday house at Ventnor, and it was reassuring to know that some things in life had not changed dramatically. For Rene and I, this short trip became something very special. It was here that I decided to propose to Rene. She accepted and we immediately went and told Tony and Ivy. Rene said to me on the trip back to Woking that she thought I might propose to her and she had already made up her mind that she wanted to marry me. Everything seemed to move a little faster in our life. One of the first things I did after arriving back home was to invite Rene's father down to the Red House Pub in Woking town centre. This was more than just a social drink. I formally asked Rene's father, Arthur, for his approval to marry his only daughter which he happily consented to.

The engagement was organised for June and the wedding ceremony was set for 13 November 1946. Our engagement was a quiet gathering for family, which included my mother, my sisters Irene, Ivy and Esther, Rene's mother and father, Mabel and Arthur, and Rene's younger brother Roy, who was still at school. Rene's two eldest brothers Reg and Ron (Digger) were still on active service overseas. I gave Rene a double diamond and single emerald engagement ring. It was late autumn and the days were quite cold by Wednesday 13 November. On this day there were no clouds in sight, the sky blue, sunny and clear. On the morning of our marriage, my mother, and Rene's parents, had been up since early morning to organise last minute preparations. The reception was to be held in Horsell Parish Hall near St Mary's Church. We kept one of the three tiers of the wedding cake for our hoped-for first child's christening, which was still a tradition during this era. The bridesmaids, Ivy, Esther, Irene and Mims, a friend of Rene's from the Cooperative office, all came to Rene's parent's house on the morning of the wedding to help her dress. I gave the bridesmaids a necklace each as a gift on the wedding day.

The Bridal party had approximately a ten minute drive to the church from her family's home at 15 West Street in Woking. Rene and her father left for St Mary's Church at approximately 1.45 pm and when they stepped out of their house, many of their neighbours came out as a mark of respect to wish them well and to see the bride in her wedding dress. Rene's dad asked their driver to take a longer circuit than originally arranged in keeping with a tradition for some people in Woking during these years, that is, to turn up at the entrance to the church a few minutes later than expected. The bridal car with Rene and her father arrived almost exactly five minutes late. They met up with the bridesmaids at the church entrance. I, my younger brother Bob (best man), and Tony Black (groomsman) were standing at the top of the aisle with the Preacher, Mr Woodard. Mendelssohn's *Wedding March* was played and Rene proceeded to walk down the aisle with her father and bridesmaids behind. Rene's dad told her at one stage to walk a little quicker – maybe he was a little nervous!

Rene and I took our marriage vows and the service went as planned. My mother, Rene and her parents and I then went to sign our marriage certificate. On the way out of St Mary's the *Wedding March* was played again and the church bells were rung. This part of the service cost a little extra, but was worth it to finish the ceremony. The weather remained fine all day and at the end of it, we set off for our two-week honeymoon on the Isle of Wight.

I will finish my recollections here apart from the following:

Still with me to some extent, I cannot concentrate on a subject for any great length of time, and sometimes only a few hours or a few weeks. This was proven to me when I attempted to restart a process of further education immediately after the war. I tried two correspondence courses but had to stop. I cannot help wondering why as my twilight years dawn upon me. I realise that I never reached my better potential, but I am still grateful to have lived a relatively healthy life, despite obvious setbacks, with the unwavering love and support of my wife, our seven sons, other family members, friends and colleagues.

Laudate Dominum – Praise the Lord

My time as a Prisoner of War of the Japanese Imperial Forces were, and remained throughout my life, a pivotal and painful episode of my time in this world. Fast-forward to the early 1970s, and nightmares and recollections of my PoW experiences, for whatever reason(s), began to haunt me again. As they became more regular and vivid, I started on the pathway to a breakdown. These were not easy times and the burden fell mostly on my beloved wife. The last few months prior to my admittance into hospital, I realised I needed help and Rene was always the first and last person at my side. This was the moment when I asked Rene to get medical assistance. Over several weeks in hospital, and with the help of specialists, I gradually made a partial recovery. For most years since this breakdown, I have continued to suffer from bouts of depression and many nights pass with little or no sleep. For better or worse, I never once thought of ever taking my own life. This would have been too traumatic for my family and, in my mind, a capitulation and final victory by my wartime enemy: the Japanese military.

My farewell wish is simply this: *I wish everyone a happy, peaceful and long life.*

Chapter 9

2015: Postscript

The Geneva Convention referred to in this biography was signed in 1929. It is this version of the Convention that covered the treatment of Prisoners of War during the Second World War, and is the predecessor of the Third Convention signed in 1949. The Empire of Japan, which did not sign the 1929 Geneva Convention, also did not treat prisoners in accordance with international agreements. The International Red Cross were denied access to Japan's Prisoners of War in Rangoon. Prisoners of War incarcerated by the Japanese had been constantly subjected to beatings, summary punishment, murder, forced labour, medical experimentation, given starvation rations and poor medical treatment.

On 19 May 1945, the United States Government, through the Swiss Legation, sent a document of protest to the then Japanese Foreign Minister, Togo, concerning 'A particularly cruel and premeditated massacre of American prisoners.' The International Military Tribunal for the Far East stated; 'this occurred on 14th December 1944 at the Prisoner of War camp above the Bay of Puerto Princesa on the Philippine Island of Palawan.'

This document included the following statement;

Such barbaric behaviour on the part of the Japanese armed forces is an offence to all civilized people. The Japanese Government cannot escape punishment for this crime. The United States Government demands that appropriate punishment be inflicted on all those who directed or took part in it.[53]

In the 2007 book *World War II*, Willmott et al write:

President Truman of the United States of America and his cabinet decided that unconditional Japanese surrender did not necessarily mean the dethronement of Emperor Hirohito. They felt that the Japanese would accept defeat more easily if Hirohito kept his position. General Douglas MacArthur was placed in charge of Japanese reconstruction. MacArthur and his advisers decided that those who had led the nation into war would be tried as war criminals, with the important exception of the Emperor himself. Under MacArthur's autocratic leadership, Japan began a transformation from a rigid, hierarchical society into a modern, pluralistic nation.

MacArthur concentrated on ensuring that Japan would emerge as an economically vibrant US ally in the Far East. The need to rebuild the Japanese economy became all the more pressing as US–Soviet relations began to deteriorate. US leaders realised that Japan would have to be self-sufficient if it were to serve as a bulwark against potential communist incursion in the Pacific. When the Cold War flared into military conflict in the Korean War (1950-53), fought between communist China and North Korea on the one hand and South Korea and the United Nations on the other, the huge boost to the Japanese economy from supplying the United States and its allies cemented its recovery.

The post-war Japanese Constitution drawn up by the Supreme Allied Commander was intended to rid Japan of the worst excesses of its reliance on tradition and to ensure that militarism would have no place in Japan's future. Many of the Japanese military implicated in the numerous atrocities on their victims throughout the Second World War and preceding the conflict were not punished. In the aftermath of the War in 1946 War Crime Trials against the Japanese were held for some of those responsible for the treatment of their former Prisoners of War. Twenty-five of the higher ranking

Japanese military were put on trial and General Tojo Hideki, the Japanese wartime Prime Minister. Seven were sentenced to hang including Hideki. Sixteen were sentenced to life imprisonment but were paroled within ten years.'[54]

With reference to Rangoon Gaol, the punishment of two senior and one of lower ranked military personnel involved in running this prison are as follows:

Captain Tazumi Motozo, Commanding Officer of Rangoon Gaol - Received 7 years' imprisonment. Motozo had also been Commandant of Changi Gaol in Singapore from April 1943 to January 1944.

Lieutenant Onishi Akio, Medical Officer, Rangoon Gaol – Sentenced to death by Hanging but later commuted to Life Imprisonment.

Superior Private Veno Koigetsu; Guard at Rangoon Gaol – Received 15 years' imprisonment[55]

The International Military Tribunal set up in 1946 in Tokyo, and almost single-handedly controlled by General Douglas MacArthur, sought to bring to trial those responsible for some of the larger massacres and atrocities under Japanese military rule, including the attack on Pear Harbour, the Rape of Nanking and the Bataan Death March. Emperor Hirohito died on 7 January 1989. Arthur Titherington in his memoirs as a former PoW of the Japanese in Formosa (now Taiwan) wrote of the Emperor that;

His escape from the judgement of his enemies was, without a doubt, politically expedient, in particular by the Americans.

Ronald Reagan, former president of the United States, stated on the occasion of Hirohito's funeral:

> *His majesty played a truly heroic role of bringing hostilities to an end.'* Titherington's reply to these sentiments was: *Mr Reagan was one of the people of an age to be available for war service to whom the principle, 'The further from the battle zone the easier it is to talk,' applied. He spent the war years 'fighting the war on the film lots of Hollywood and sleeping in his own bed every night.'*[56]

Some Japanese people have never fully accepted responsibility for the atrocities perpetrated against their country's Prisoners of War and civilian internees. However in August 1995 the Guardian reported that sixty years after the end of the war a resolution in the Japanese Parliament apologised for its wartime atrocities.[57] In 1998 Emperor Akihito, born on 23 December 1933 and the fifth child of Emperor Hirihito of Japan, was invested with the Order of the Garter by Queen Elizabeth II during a state visit to the United Kingdom.

This, to many former PoWs and their families, was considered an insult and an act of betrayal given the enormity of sacrifice, loss and pain endured by so many thousands of men and women in fighting for King and Empire. For much of the wider public, opinion with regards to wartime atrocities committed on prisoners, their sentiments have evolved into a case of 'forgive but never forget'. Many others might find that they are never able to forgive.

It was not until 15 August 2005, the anniversary of VJ Day, that the then Japanese Prime Minister, Mr Koizumi, acknowledged the 'huge damage and suffering' Japan had caused in the Second World War. For many of the former PoWs who suffered at the hands of the Japanese, and those who have now passed away, these sentiments were a disgrace and a sham. It was far too little and far too late. As Lord Russell of Liverpool unequivocally wrote:

Many of those who survived captivity will carry its marks upon them for the rest of their lives, and for many more the expectation of life has been considerably shortened. Many thousands of civilian internees died during captivity, and many others have prematurely died since, wasted by disease. There are some who will never recover from their experiences of Japanese occupation, and will remain, until their dying day, broken in body and warped in mind. All this they owe to the 'Knights of Bushido'.[58]

My father, who intimated at times that he might one day be able to forgive, but would never forget his experiences, nor relinquish all of his hatred of the Japanese during that period in time, reiterated a little of Lord Russell's sentiments in 1995 on the fiftieth anniversary of the ending of the war when he said;

From the moment Brigadier Hobson made his announcement to us that we were free men this was true in one sense only. For many former PoWs of the Japanese Imperial Forces, we remained captive to the atrocities committed on us that could never be eradicated from our minds and bodies; at least not until we shall leave this mortal world. Not only were horrific memories irremediably assimilated into our post war 'personality' but there remained the outwardly visual physically reminders. Apart from my damaged toe nails from being tortured in 1943 when in solitary, I also have several scars from jungle sores which have been a constant reminder of a tiny part of the diabolical treatment I suffered in that (Rangoon) *gaol.*

As to the atrocities committed by Japanese forces during this war a short quote from Ray Slattery, I feel, is relevant; 'Not even the new-found friendships and marriages of convenience between modern governments, can wipe it out.'[59]

These sentiments echo to some degree with those of Colonel MacKenzie (Dr) who wrote nine years after his own PoW experiences in Rangoon.

I wish to sound no historical note about a 'Yellow Peril' but I do implore men of good-will everywhere to consider the facts and, when they have done so to ask themselves the question: 'Are we sure that the Japanese are now as democratic as they claim to be and have they indeed been converted to a belief in international co-operation and fundamental human rights?' If they have, it is certainly the quickest, the most remarkable and the most unexpected change of outlook in the history of the world.[60]

*   *   *

My father wanted to believe that post-war generations of Japanese people are not of the same character as their forefathers who committed incalculable acts of inhumane violence. My father was the embodiment of a compassionate and generous man who knew what cruelty and privation embodied. I have attempted to research and write this book in as honest an appraisal as I am able to, given the simple fact that, as a son of one of the thousands of former Prisoners of War of the Imperial Japanese Forces, I witnessed first hand much of the life-long post-war torment that my father had to manage; of many times a 'shattered' man, and the impacts of this on his personal life and my mother in particular. For much of his life after 1945, Bill was prescribed medication to manage a number of conditions including depression, chronic insomnia, anxiety and physical pain as a result of the ill-treatment he received in Rangoon Gaol. For over sixty years, professional advice and support came predominantly from psychiatrists, general practitioners and podiatrists. Having said this, it is impossible to calculate the physical and emotional support from Bill's devoted wife during this period. How does one measure, over the seven decades since the end of the war, be it quantitatively or qualitatively, the consequences of what my father and his fellow PoWs and civilian internees were subjected to?

My father never left a morsel of food on his plate with any meal he ate, nor a drop of fluid in anything he had to drink. Even though it would usually take Bill longer than any other person during a meal to slowly and meticulously consume his food down to the last visible crumb, we understood what turmoil his thoughts were going through. I sometimes think to this day that, with almost every mouthful of food my father swallowed, he often inwardly and silently recalled those two years of imprisonment and impoverishment, pain and persecution, hunger and humiliation, death and disease and terror and tyranny that he lived through and somehow managed to survive.

My father divulged fragments of his 'Encounter with Nippon' as a Prisoner Of War following his breakdown in 1974. I am thus reminded of a line from a novel by one of my father's favourite authors and close with this quote:

Have I yet to learn that the hardest and best-borne trials are those which are never chronicled in any earthly record, and are suffered every day!

Charles Dickens.

*   *   *

Bibliography

Information used for this book has been obtained from various sources including the personal recollections, wartime documents and books of William Albert Tate, his wife Irene, their seven sons and other family members. I want to thank a number of organisations for information including the Marine Corps Heritage Foundation, the Imperial War Museum (London), the RAF Museum in Hendon and the National Archives at Kew. I sincerely apologise for any misrepresentations or mistakes on my behalf.

1. *Daily Mail*, Saturday October 18, 2008, p. 33.
2. http://telegraph.uk.history.rafbombercommand
3. Bomber Command Association, News letter, No. 67 Spring 2014.
4. Falconer, J., *RAF Bomber Crewmen*, Shire Publications, 2010 U.K. pp. 38–41.
5. http://www.raf.mod.uk/history/38squadron.cfm
6. http://www.diggerhistory.info/pages_air_support/ww2_allied/ wellington.htm
7. *DEKHO*: Winter Issue 2014 p. 20.
8. http://www.elsham.pwp.blueyoder.co.uk
9. Thompson, J., *Forgotten Voices of Burma*, Ebury Press, 2010 UK. p. 46.
10. Beevor, A., *The Second World War*, Weidenfeld & Nicholson, 2012, UK. p. 128.
11. Bayly, C and Harper, T., *Forgotten Wars: The End of Britain's Asian Empire*, Penguin Books 2008. pp. 142–3.
12. Thompson, J., *Forgotten Voices of Burma*, Ebury Press, 2010 U.K. p. 46.
13. *ibid*.
14. The Flying Mule, Historical Notes: *The Wellington Bomber*, 2007 U.S.A.
15. Beevor, A., *The Second World War*, Weidenfeld & Nicholson, 2012 U.K. p. 466.
16. *ibid* p. 557

17. Willmott, H.P., Cross, R., & Messenger., *World War II*, DK Publishing 2007.
18. Bayly, C and Harper, T., *Forgotten Wars: The End of Britain's Asian Empire*, Penguin Books 2008 England pp. 15–19.
19. *FULCRUM* Japanese Labour Camp Survivors Association of Great Britain Newsletter, Issue No. 69 November 2002 p. 9 'Extracts from '*Gold Warriors*' *(The Covert History of Yamashita's Gold)* by Seagrave, S & P., Bowstring Books.
20. *FULCRUM* Japanese Labour Survivors Association of Great Britain Newsletter, Issue No. 69 November 2002 p. 7 '*So Farewell to Akihito*'.
21. Thompson, J., *Forgotten Voices of Burma*, Ebury Press, 2010 U.K. pp. 16–17.
22. Bayly, C and Harper, T., *Forgotten Wars: The End of Britain's Asian Empire*, Penguin Books 2008.
23. Thompson, J., *Forgotten Voices of Burma*, Ebury Press, 2010 U.K. p. 308
24. Titherington, A., *Kinkaseki One Day at a Time*, Covos Day Books, 2000 South Africa. p 120 Refers to a quote from Prof. Taid O'Connor, '*The Menace of Japan.*' (1936).
25. Stanley, P., (Dr) *The Australian Magazine*: 60th Anniversary Series WW II, Part 7, p. 17.
26. Australian Broadcasting Corporation, DVD, *Britain at War*, 2010 Part 10: Burma.
27. http://en.wikipedia.or/wiki/Arakan_Campaign 1942-3
28. http://www.ourstory.info/library/4_ww2/VB/Burma.html
29. Hudson, L.H. (Wg Cdr)., *The Rats of Rangoon*, Arrow Books, 1989 U.K. pp. 31–2 & 58–9.
30. Stibbe, P.G., *Return via Rangoon*, Leo Cooper, London, 1995 London pp. 101–2.
31. Hudson, L.H., (Wg Cdr)., *The Rats of Rangoon*, Arrow Books, 1989 U.K. p. 59.
32. Coubrough, CRL., *Memories of a Perpetual Second Lieutenant*, 1987 Great Britain p. 101.
33. Slattery, R., *Samurai: The Sword of Horror*, Horwitz Publications Inc. Pty Ltd, 1965 London pp. 126–7.
34. MacKenzie, K.P., (Colonel, Dr)., *Operation Rangoon Jail*, Christopher Johnson, 1954 London p. 74.

35. Beevor, A., *The Second World War*, Weidenfeld & Nicholson, 2012 U.K. p. 60.
36. *FULCRUM* Japanese Labour Camp Survivors Association of Great Britain, Newsletter, Issue No. 69, November 2002 p. 12.
37. Stibbe, P.G., *Return via Rangoon*, Leo Cooper, London, 1995 London pp. 197–9.
38. MacKenzie, K.P., (Colonel, Dr)., *Operation Rangoon Jail*, Christopher Johnson, 1954 London pp. 87–8.
39. The Sunday Telegraph, "*Don't Flout Geneva Convention*", 1 October 2006.
40. *Far East*, Companion Journal to *The Prisoner of War*. The Official Journal of the Prisoners of War Department of the Red Cross and St John War Organisation, St James's Palace, London, SWI. Vol. I. No. 10, September 1945 p. 9.
41. MacKenzie, K.P. (Colonel, Dr)., *Operation Rangoon Jail*, Christopher Johnson, 1954 London p. 106.
42. Stibbe, P.G., *Return via Rangoon*, Leo Cooper, 1995 London p. 109.
43. *ibid* pp. 116–17.
44. *ibid* p. 180.
45. *ibid* p. 108.
46. MacKenzie, K.P., (Colonel, Dr), *Operation Rangoon Jail*, Christopher Johnson, 1954 London pp. 87–9.
47. *ibid* pp. 102–4.
48. *ibid* p. 97.
49. Australian Broadcasting Corporation, DVD, *Britain at War*, 2010 Part 10: Burma.
50. Hudson, L., (Wg. Cdr.), *The Rats of Rangoon*, Arrow Books, 1989 U.K. p. 210.
51. *ibid*.
52. Slattery, R., *Samurai: The Sword of Horror*, Horwitz Publications Inc. Pty Ltd, 1965 London p.11.
53. Russell, (Lord) of Liverpool., *The Knights of Bushido*, Corgi Books, 1967 Great Britain pp. 95–8.
54. Willmott, H.P., Cross, R., & Messenger, C., *World War II*, DK Publishing, 2007 New York pp. 302–3.

55. Hudson, L., (Wg. Cdr.), *The Rats of Rangoon*, Arrow Books, 1989 U.K. p.128 Information obtained from the War Office Files, Public Records Office Kew, London. 2012. Sourced from War Crime Trials.
56. Titherington, A, *Kinkaseki One Day at a Time*, Covos Day Books, 2000 South Africa pp. 235–8.
57. www.guardian.com>world>japan
58. Russell, (Lord) of Liverpool, *The Knights of Bushido*, Corgi Books, 1967 Great Britain pp. 163–71.
59. Slattery, R., *Samurai: The Sword of Horror*, Horwitz Publications Inc. Pty Ltd, 1965 London p. 59.
60. MacKenzie, K.P., (Colonel, Dr), *Operation Rangoon Jail*, Christopher Johnson, 1954 London p. 192.